solitude

a collection of awakenings rendered in poetry

by Matt Pelicano

Averlune Press, Inc.

Averlune Press, Inc.
www.Averlune.com

Matt Pelicano
www.MattPelicano.com

Cover Photograph of Reynisdrangar Cliffs, Iceland
by Joey Pelicano
www.JoeyPelicano.com

Publisher's Note: This is a work of fiction. Names, characters, places, and incidents are a product of the author's imagination. Locales and public names are sometimes used for atmospheric purposes. Any resemblance to actual people, living or dead, or to businesses, companies, events, institutions, or locales is completely coincidental.

Summary: *solitude* is a collection of poems written within the span of nine months. During this time of discovery, the poet found himself living in a place that held great significance from his youth, a place whose present situation did not always easily reconcile with its past. In the quiet of his thoughts and the solitude of hidden moments, the poet picked up the threads he had long ago set aside, in an effort to reconnect past with present, and better understand the tapestry his life had become.

solitude seeks to forge connections between ancestry and destiny, life and death, questions and answers, gratitude and the deepening of love. Though not written with the intention of presenting a collection of common themes, a commonality runs through the selections included in this compilation of poems. Perhaps that commonality is simply the poet's recognition that all things are connected and even the passage of time flows along a riverbed of cohesive purpose. In *solitude*, we are often better equipped to hear and understand such purpose. Within these pages, the poet learned to listen.

1. Poetry – American / General

ISBN/SKU: 9798218146665
ISBN Complete: 979-8-218-14666-5
Publication Date: 2/15/2023

solitude/Matt Pelicano. -- 1st ed.
ISBN 979-8-218-14666-5

for my parents

Table of Contents

Ode to a June bug

armor-clad
in stealth-angular
iridescence,
you bristle beneath
a slicked-back
mullet of prickly
unpleasantries;
copper goggles,
like mesh-covered speakers,
tempt me to touch
the dry-durable
of your rugged-eyes;
the thought thrills
and disgusts
my curiosity;
i shall resist
this juvenile urge;

unwitting courier,
your body sparkles
with stowaways;
powder from sticky,
sweet tendrils;
nature's excessive insistence
upon propagation;
efficiencies of scale
writ large
across the blushing cheeks
of chaste blossom and bud;

i feel the arresting snag
of your barbed
and thorny stalks;
hollow limbs
of appalling;
like miniature,
charred grasshoppers;
with wings of empty
stained glass calmes –
dangling lead frames, unsightly;
the humming buzz of fishnet
holds aloft this body
by sheer force of rage;

how dare these carrion feet,
these dunghill boots
tread, trampling roughshod
over innocence, pure and petaled?
do they not foul
the very perfume of the air?
or are they not –
upon close examination -
less ghastly grim
and much more
truly fair?

Elusive Bluebird

the rain has rusted
and run corrosive,
staining breast
and breeches
reddish-brown;
with creamy jodhpurs,
pulled-up tight
around a belly
more fit
for a country squire;
you are no gentleman
of leisure; there is too much
work to be done;

if i held you in my hands,
trembling at the wondrous
of your tiny soul,
would you chalk them
powder blue?
like an old shed
of corrugated
and weatherworn,
your dull silver primer
peaks through;

echoes of ancestry,
reptilian feathers
hide scaled feet;
dinosaur blood
through thimble heart,

coursing more rapidly
than any raptor
might run;
your genius
is for survival,
their ancient race
is done;

sweet bluebird,
i name you
an omen
on wings;
and give thanks
for the joy
each fortunate
sighting
brings.

Dandelion

a galaxy of downy stars
bursts softness
o'er celestial fields;
around pin cushion
suns, seedlings
arrange themselves
in orbits of affection;
their backs
to the wind;
their faces
in rapt attention;

through veins
of green and fibrous,
milk, as thick
as chilled reluctance, creeps
with silent determination;
cooling the toes
of those bent
on reckless flight;
their restless spirits
covet nature's heights;

the lightest touch –
nay, softer still -
the mere inkling
of a sigh
caresses every strand
like timid expectation;
as a maiden's hair

is stirred
by tender breath
from lover's lips,
no tremor
proves too soft
for sensitive souls;
once freed,
who can say
where captive hearts
might go?

At the Withering

bruised-heart
and sorrowful;
with whose eyes
do you weep?
dripping purple
from sockets stained
with vacant age,
your face wears hollow
like a sad and sullen mood;

may i gaze
into your secrets
of yellow taffeta
and grey?
hidden beneath four petals
draped like modest starfish
over bulbous and pure;
i, too, have ripened
well beyond my years;

in desperate arms,
you catch and hold
the sweet spring rains
and offer hope
upon the wayward,
fickle wind;
snatching chance
from greedy lifeless;
scattering splendor
on the fields;

your tiny touches,
kindness unrestrained;

bruised and broken heart,
i am no fair-weather friend;
i will not close myself
against the shadows,
dark and cold;
but rather,
sit with you in silence;
wrap your trembling
in my warm;
and keep your colors
vibrant,
as we grow old.

Hydrangea in Autumn

a fistful of yellow;
this heartful of wings;
on a twig bent
and bowed beneath
a flock of birds
of paradise; tail-feathers,
like streamers
tied to tricycle-bars;
peddling joy
in the giddy sunshine;
all contrast is lost
in the bright glare of blissful;

before a backdrop
of green and blue,
spattered like paint
upon a tarpaulin;
the sky sets,
dry and crusted,
against the coming rain;
i scrape, to no avail;
i will not use this day's
spent canvas
again;

how carefully
the sunlight caresses
every petal;
inviting each,
by name,

to open
(as a woman's heart –
vulnerable to her lover's touch);
setting free
that which winter's harshness
had enslaved;

i guide her forehead,
and rest my own
against this tender branch,
inhaling the bliss
of spring's first kiss;
the warmth of morning softness;
the breath of fragrant dew;
the colors
which compose
the fragile flower
of you.

Birdsong in the Garden

what bird is this
that calls through me,
from somewhere deep
among the hidden,
high above the seen?

i'd never heard
its voice before;
the gravel in the grip
of its gizzard;
the broken in the slack
of its beak;
its throat of slashed
and tattered
bleeds birdsong
like grief;
the morning
cannot hide
her stern displeasure;

nearby, blue jays
creak like witches
astride rusted garden gates;
awash in tortured incantations;
withering wrought iron
with wicked words
and spells unintelligible;

i pause to parse
meaning from inane;

poor, blue devils –
lacking self,
they have no sense
to see the forest
of loud ridiculous
for the slow cacophony
of trees;

and where has this
peter gone to?
the titmouse cries,
desperate, aloud;
thrice in panicked repetition;
she paints the sunrise grey
with bare-hopeful song;
as, between blossomed boughs -
carefree and unaffected –
the plump chicka-dee-dee-dee-dee-dee
knits joyful from taut strands
of scarcely awake,
until, at last,
lost peter is found;

once more,
i feel it slap the sky,
cracking wide the sunrise
like eggs against
a slow-lightening skillet;
both sound and imagery
startle the sensitive finches at play;
all of nature halts to hear
that which cannot belong:
the strange and echoing strains
of this, my soul's birdsong.

let us create a space

let us create a space;
a hallowed-out hollow;
an emptiness overflowing
with love,
in which kindness
never knows regret;
a safe haven
where the rashness
of vulnerability
never falls to ruin;
where we might
bind ourselves
amid the tangles
of quiet freedom;
and demand nothing
more than the precious
privilege of exceeding
one another
in out-loving
the other;
for, in truth as pure
as blessings from above,
there could never be
another one to love.

these days belong

these days belong
to tokens, small;
to toothbrushes
cuddling in a common cup;
to clothing in cabinets,
blankets and pillows,
and cats everywhere;
to all things finding
their tidy home;
to love's absurdities
of two heads and hearts
asleep on two separate pillows
not two miles apart;
to picnics shared
on carpets, bare;
to seedlings encased
in greeting cards;
to gifts of kindness,
and gratitude;
for a thousand tiny
flowers you've strewn
throughout my home;
to happiness together,
and longing when alone;
to stolen moments, stolen kisses,
two hands clasped, concealed by tabletops,
belying that which smiles betray;
speaking that which words dare not;
yes, these days belong to such as these,
and, for now, these are enough for me.

Route 31

from this room of unlikely,
where ended
all that ever was,
the sound of transit rises
from the road below;

the incessant rudeness
ebbs and flows
like an angry ocean
of mechanized and tiresome;
with my ear cupped
to this seashell
of doppler unending,
i wonder where it is they all flow;

(sometimes, i imagine these strangers
conspiring to drive me to madness,
but malice is rarely so organized);

it isn't the ink-roller padding
of tires blotting asphalt;
nor the whistling
of their wake,
a loose-lipped hissing
through half-clenched teeth;

rather, it is the fury of foolishness
as it belches, full-bellied
and grease-stained,
from growling guts

of toxic stupidity;

i find forbearing willful folly
trickier by the minute;
more distasteful
with each passing year;
call me cantankerous,
this alone might i bear;

and i ponder (overmuch),
how do they see themselves?
for are we not
all cast in molds
of our mind's own making?

is it them against the world?
or simply, an iconoclastic smashing
of the delicate porcelain of peace?
we assert our freedoms
against the common good,
to the imprisonment of all;

the rain falls like springtime,
feminine and cordial;
a mother without preference
among her brood;
tiny, dusty splatters
lick the asphalt clean,
and lend an endless,
sizzling snare
to the drum thrumming
of wheels on seams.

death is (would that it were not)

death is (would that it were not)
but a blind corner;
out of sight, out of time,
but always
in the alleys of my mind;
crowded queues
of those who came before;
they fill this room, evermore;

demanding, 'do you believe
what you believe?
or are we all
but shadows and dreams?

shadows and dreams...
nay, so much more;

for, i refuse to live
in a world
where any and all
that is good
could be lost;

i will believe,
i *will to* believe
it could never be,
at all and any cost.

The un-common man

these hands rest awhile,
just long enough for prayer;
laying aside their labors
of love; their weights
of worry; they carry
in their flesh
the scars of providence;

the thick, knotted sinews;
the gnarled, arthritic joints
are well at home
with the Savior's own
wounds; for He binds all ills,
with torn, disfigured hands;

see how the left thumb
throbs purple, with every hammer
stroke swung wide;
every reflexive curse
that escaped pursed lips,
is now cast
at the foot of the cross;
one more splinter
in the crossbeam;

with head bowed;
and neck furrowed
by sun and wind,
rain and care;
a lifetime of exposure

is veiled against the eyes of Heaven;
man has, of old, sought amongst
too few fig leaves for the sewing;

on the leg of tan Carhartts,
a twisted loop sags,
stretched and soiled
by every tool used
to bruise the hide
of poverty; stained by
every teardrop of toil
that moistened
the dough of daily bread;

standing, as though astride
the back of days interminable,
nights too brief;
these legs praise grateful
for the law of Sabbath rest;
and bend to duck the linteled gate
the humble enter best;

a grey thicket muffles
the din of the world's inane yammering;
barring entry to those ears
which long only to hear of peace;
the prosperity of a good conscience;
the promise of a life yet to come;

encircling his finger, a solitary treasure
gleams in the warmth
of the stained-glass sun;
a reminder of the one for whom
his deeds of life and
feats of love are done.

My love at prayer

sighs and whispers,
let us speak
no more;
our eyes know
what our hearts
long to say;

and when we kiss,
we speak
a sign-language
of the lips;
a miracle of Braille
on moistened fingertips;
no need to smudge
this raised
and textured silence;

your eyes are unfathomed
inkwells, writing reams
of verse upon the parchment
of my heart; each word,
a reflection; each word,
bare truth; composing
happy endings for all
the chapters of our youth;
i can conceive of
no greater resolution
than our love;

there can be no more-

profound subject
than your body
draped in prayer;
with none, but God, watching,
i see the posture of your simplicity;
i taste the incense of your faith;
i long to stain my lips red
in solemn communion;

these beads,
polished smooth
by prayerful fingers,
like pearl-drop tears
from porcelain statues;
the black ash of your hair,
spread wide like robes
of sack cloth and penitent;
but you have no sins left, my love;
your innocence was too chaste
for such to endure; no fault
can long persist in one
whose love is pure.

bleeding humanity

bleeding humanity,
i love thee;
in all the disfigured
of your every self-infliction;
i see myself
in the wounded wreckage,
declaring all is well,
when it couldn't be
further from the
subjectivity of all things
(would that we knew the truth);

how i am tempted
to stand apart,
as if there were a platform
upon which i might sit
and cease, awhile, to be a man;
but i belong;
and you to me,
the same;

in every utterance of People,
i am enclosed;
in every They,
is referenced Us;
in every Man,
i stand accused;
and in the eyes of so many,
i am guilty
until proven culpable;

but who can blame them?
for i, too, have lost
my innocence;

bleeding humanity,
i pity thee,
as a man laments himself;
and will not judge thee
as accursed,
lest i should thereby
judge myself.

where do the days go

where do the days go
when their lives
are all spent?
and the hours bleed
minutes to seconds;
and moments drip sunset
into pools of cool evening;
when all flows into lakes
of forgotten, what valley
could cradle such depths?

where lies the boundary
between daylight
and evening?
between now
and becoming?
between not yet
and been?
i think *imperceptible*
was invented
for just such a riddle as this;
in a world so sifted
and sorted by science,
i rejoice in the vague of it all;

where does night
acquire its mystery?
surely, darkness is
no cloak of undiscovered;
no shroud of unknown;

all remains
as was there
in the light,
sound reason has shown;
but, if confounding is the veil
setting night from day, apart,
then, surely, there's no deeper mystery
than that of the human heart.

southern storm

southern storm
thunders rage
against my panes,
with fists
of gushing tantrums,
dense as the flesh
of sodden fruit;
fury runs,
black and ragged,
down naked streets;

through my open window,
the heavy air squeezes
her thick thighs,
sitting astride
my heaving chest,
filling the night
with cold remorse;
even the gasping ground
gulps mouthfuls
of muddy despair;

the thunderheads
seem stern
beyond reckoning;
their brooding minds
glow pink with humid discontent;
these are not tears they shed,
but the rabid slavering
of feckless raving;

what tragedy befell
to pervert such pure souls,
none can say;

lightning stamps mayhem
across the face of the sky;
like razor burn
dragged over dry skin,
it flays my spine raw;
even the tree frogs
scream dismay,
each raindrop falling
like a spike to impale
their thin, wet skins –
like so many vile trophies;
chaos spins cruelty
in careless stampedes;

but listen…

count the miles
as they widen
between thunder
and light,
i'm certain of one thing:
i will not sleep again
this night.

scales of Leviathan

scales of Leviathan
collect along the shore,
sloughed off
and cast to the four winds;
the sea serpent sheds winter
without a shred of sentiment,
without a moment
of reticulated regret;

slithering among the stones,
the lake waters search
sand and sinew for news
of approaching spring:
here, a seedling sprouts;
there, an earthworm stretches
and yawns long, lanky
swallows of midday;

with slow, rhythmic shrugs,
the water wriggles free
of debris from shoulders stiff
with winter's cold constraints;
each sunrise shrinks
the diminishing pile;
each sunset delays
its departure awhile;

where water and ether meet,
threads of gold
draw tight the seam

between heaven and earth;
a scar of sunlight
upon the wrinkled face of day;
the horizon softens
like watercolor
pigments in the rain;

mountains of shapeless
spread wide above the waves,
surrendering life and breath
to the rending hands
of the wind; each formless stone
becoming one with the sky;
faint smudges of enormous
context guide the wandering eye;

in the near-silent grind of fractured,
where fault finds fissures
rough with untamed purpose,
i regard this old lake
more gravely
than she gives
thought
to me.

this night is blessed

this night is blessed;
unfurled in splendor,
bedecked by grace,
she kneels to her Maker;
receiving the bloody
smear of belonging,
at the end of this
long, trying day;
it is enough to belong,
when love is the bearer;
it is enough to bear,
when belonging's the goal;
not a moment too soon,
she is crossed
in benediction;
she is signed
by the sky;
then dips
below the waters
of baptismal horizons,
where daylight
will find her
born again;
a new creation;
the morrow,
where once only
sorrow could speak
of what dawned before;
this night is now blessed,
ever-loved, evermore.

Flight delayed

knit lace
of black, bitter satin
slips like innocence
down curves of glass
and willing, clothing
each sip in elegant
white remains
of Guinness; while
the radio plays *Cracklin'*
Rosie, an anthem to all
that is coarse and common
and chauvinistic, just one
of many '70s more;
why do i equate
the decade of my birth
with so little
that is good
and clean
and hygienic?
the hangover
after the revolution;
best at home in Vegas,
shirt open, hair-framed
medallion of gold; kitsch
is the word i'll choose;
what do i expect
from an airport bar?
what emptiness i find
apart from where you are.

the man seated next to me

the man
seated
next to me
is at home
nowhere;

                              i wonder
                              if he reads
                              what i write
                              about him,
                              for he stares
                              at me without
                              blinking;

i lean back,
stretching arms,
and shoulders,
and chest,
and credibility,
in a primal show
of strength;

                              thank God
                              this softness lives
                              inside imposing;
                              pray, i never have cause
                              to use it; the pen is deadlier,
                              but these fists
                              are fictional at best;

he spreads wide
his bits, and bobs,
and clippings
of scrap;

stacks high
his collection
of clinking coins;

i'm sure he works
a paper route:
do people still walk
such outdated,
analogs as this?

something selfish
inside of me
hopes they do;
for what could be
more useless
than a writer?

he hunches
over his wares,
like a gargoyle
guarding all he has
received on God's
green earth;

i pity him,
without cause;
hunched, as i am,
over my words
like a paper gargoyle
guarding all i have
left of myself

against the scattering
winds of late afternoon.

i do not wish to live

i do not wish to live
for this self;
i have wandered
such barren before;

those are lands
of illusion;
those, endless
processions of bleak;
a glaring mirage
in a desert
of arid lies;

such paths lead,
concentrically,
inward;
ever smaller,
ever fading;
until naught
but i remains;

there, i feasted
my fill
of such empty;

and, empty,
i would have
remained;

every injustice

i wielded
was loss;
every hurt
i inflicted
was mine;

every word
spoken in anger,
a curse
upon my head;
a failure
of strength;
a victory
of weakness;

and, living thus,
what did i gain?
are lessons,
once learned,
always worth
so much pain?

black trees

black trees,
thick with raucous;
dripping leaf, seed,
stem, and fowl;
below the bending,
bobbing branches,
i cringe with terror,
head down and
sheltering from
the stormcrow;

the evening breeze,
like mother's hand, unseen,
cups boughs in bouncing
baby lullabies; or like

a wild, white-haired,
rouge-faced conductress
taming unchained melodies
for the masses from
the throats of a murder
of orchestral crows;

sprinkled like saltpeter
in a peppery wound,
red-winged blackbirds
wear twin stripes
like corporals proud;
bright gashes
against a necrotic

smudge of crow;
rags of black gauze
flutter like heartbeats
in the wind;

the evening snow,
a contrast in drab;
a study in Poe,
the tree creaks ominous,
"nevermore, nevermore;"

while i, with camera eye,
seek to steal
the blackbird's soul;
when off fly
bashful ravens,
loathe to
lend me
their likeness awhile;

but, up in the shuddering tree,
released at last from cramped
and swarming throng,
the red-winged blackbirds pause;

in silent surrender,
born aloft
on the unaltered air,
they yield
their winter souls
to me;
a contrast
in graceful poise;
a study
in peaceful ecstasy.

bronzed warrior

bronzed warrior
clad in fear,
upon what do you graze,
among these leaves,
but ripe apprehension?

amid the clatter of hinged
jaws and mechanical mandibles,
my dread is no match for your size;

these wings are but quills of purple,
piercing ink pots of fatal iridescence,
writing woe upon the cringing sky;

how nature fashioned you so small,
in skin of crustaceous steel,
i cannot guess; i've seen
her landscaped hands, her seismic
fingertips; they are too grand
for details such as you;

scorched in umber, you bear
the scars of battle; every feature,
the very genius of weaponry;

i plead no contest, on my knees;
i will withdraw
and yield to you these leaves.

Early blooms of lavender

with fingerless lace,
the wind lifts the veil
from your chaste
and blushing; violet
so becomes your every mood,
as lavender wears springtime
in the afternoon;
though summer is best suited
to evening;

crowning tiny evergreens,
you startle the mind;
your face, not unlike a velvet
pill bug, or some alien lobster tail;
i cannot decide if ugly
looks good on you,
or if beauty is truly
in the eye of the beholder;

the sunless sky throws
fistfuls of grey and overcast,
crowding the morning air
with needless brooding;
i hate when she gets like this;
more inconsolable than
a mourning dove on monday,
she plants the helpless meadow
thick with melancholy;

with thumb and forefinger,

i pinch proud heads
from hairy necks,
watching them fall dead
at my feet; rolling, face up,
they stare back in cold dismay;
but what is it i might say?
it would surely be small
consolation for them to know
that blooming too soon
often means forfeiting growth.

solitude

solitude;
cold as drifted desolation
on a lake where anguish
goes to die; the wind wails
hostile, with frozen flagrance,
she probes the secret spaces
where, once, my body clung to life;

i liquify; eyes tear at the touch
of harsh winter's dry breath;
she handles all things tender
too roughly; even my nose runs
to outstrip her; when only spring
could hope to win;

a torso stands, limbless,
leafless, lifeless in the wrinkled fist
of brutal waters, once-liquid,
now stone; strangling the stifled
struggle; stripped bare
beneath translucent ice;
plundered modesty,
the final affront;

ringing the shore like heartless
spectators, shrubs bristle wild
with morbid curiosity, straining
their broken necks to glimpse
the captive corpse;

my gorge rises at the sight
of so much grim despondent;
so much bleak and barren;
for, even the mountains
surrender to the scene;
while, beneath the biting snow,
one, hopeful crocus
strives to break free.

among your tiny hearts

among your tiny hearts,
bloodied by countless
abrasions, quivering, raw
to the feather's touch,
angels swim
in unseen currents;

i cannot help but hold your buds;
to feel their imperceptible pulsing;
to grasp their internal vigor
between thumb and forethought;
to find some of that which
mortality molders to grey;

you are no stranger
to the scorching sun;

you are no captive
to the witless winds;

and yet, you are no more jaded
than nature's own true innocence;
for patience is your strength;

when spring is belied
by sudden frost,
you draw yourself
around yourself, better,
yourself to preserve;

when summer comes, full fury,
blazing heedless
in the crumbling sky,
you answer his impertinence,
full-fruited in self-sufficient grandeur,
with the quiet calm of a newborn;

for you are a slave to no one,
fair daughter of the earth.

the ragged earth is razor-burned

the ragged earth is razor-burned;
stiff stubble chafes the cheek of the wind,
caressing, as she does, her lover's face;
the sun sets soonest, these days; 5 o'clock
shadows are lengthening;

among summer's severed stalks,
blackhead crows, like moles
marring unblemished faces, burden
the morning air with their rowdy,
strident screeches; would that the sky
might, pillowing, smother them whole;

in laundry heaps of soiled and dismal,
winter's raiment huddles fast
against the warmth of a fuller
who seeks to bleach them bare;

who knows what treasures lurk
within the folds and pockets
of core-frozen snowbanks: shopping
carts and sundry lives swept up
by indiscriminate snowplows;
a heart, once thawed,
reveals all things;

the field, too, is a graveyard of markers;
rows and aisles of unforced perspective;
husks of withered skin; ears of gnawed
and toothless; unfit to swallow by any

but the gluttonous mud;
i lose my eye
inside a maze of amazement;
who plants with such precision?
who masters the indifferent ground?

is this not a metaphor?
is it not like a simile?
that i might walk
so far afield
to master
the seasons
within me.

i hold your hand

i hold your hand
in places
you have not yet been;
in ways
you have not yet walked;
in days
you have never spent with me;

what distance drives apart,
casting chasms
of yearning
in its wake,
my mind fills
with phantoms;
until your sweet hand
can take their place.

the mountain breathes with lungs

the mountain breathes with lungs
of foothill and floodplain;
upon its slopes,
fir trees spread wide
their feathered fingers,
gathering hope sopping
white with purity;

a river of relentless mist flows,
three feet atop the matted floor;
weaving, wafting, weeping its
sluggish way around all in its
path; fox and hare drown
in gossamer veils - hung
lifeless above the gurgling ground;

grey run the watercolor hues,
down dense windowpanes
of sky and unbroken; vistas
spread like bridal trains,
less costly
but more assured;

the sullen landscape
wears upheaval,
a mad portrait
of disproportionate;
rendered in Neo-Topsyturvism,
the sky surges
like turbid seawater,

while earthen tides
reclaim the fallen leaves;

along mystic pathways,
geese cry desperate
in the creeping fog;
their feet ache
to feel the sponge
of safe landing;
never were souls
less suited for flight
than waterfowl
above this fluid plain;

oh, how i fear the sun has died;
how pale he looks in yonder sky.

Coming home

was it just
that you were sleeping?
awaiting the change of season?
attentive to the slightest hues
of meaning as they shift colors
beneath a muted morning's smile?
was it this
and nothing more
that caught your gaze
for a while?

was it just
that i was lacking?
digging bones
from grey earth;
resurrecting those
who had earned
a good, fair rest?
grappling with the bastard
present, a child who bears
so little resemblance to its past?
did i truly believe
that such things as these
were made to last?

was it just
that you were speaking,
at a loss to find the answers
that would soothe
the sad insatiable

within me?
what right had i
to demand
you render an account?
what right had i
to try
and understand?
you are not the souls
of those who came before;
you are witless,
puerile earth,
the ragged remnants
of their land.

OLGCC

what is this place?
these four walls
enclosing subtle sacred?

this exhalation of divine?
this scent of incense lingering?

these throbbing wicks,
pulsing out prayers
in rhythmic supplication?

what is this space
wherein actors play
the role of their lives?

where footlights
reveal their sufferings
of tragic renown?

their ecstasies
of simple obscurity?

their everyday common,
if such trifles exist?

is it the quiet
of empty i hear?

or the silence of unbroken
ages rolling like foothills

to the velvet sea?

or is it just the silence
inside of me?

what is this stillness
begetting reverence,
begetting mystic,
begetting awe
from shapeless numinous
in hearts of earthen -
bound to remember
that we are dust,
and to dust
we shall return?

what are these faces
looking back at me,
if not lessons to be learned?

The poet's paradox

look, the curtain is drawn;
the veil is parted;
all is revealed,
though vulnerability cripples
the tongue with its black tar effluvium;

i am laid bare to your gazes;
i submit to scrutiny, for the sake
of one fleeting moment of raw
understanding between strangers;

one instant of connection,
in which might be found
the recognition
of a shared humanity;

it's a tiptoeing tightrope dance,
to fashion reckless candor
while preserving privacy
from being dashed against
the stones of coarse calumny;

the ceaseless tug-of-war
longs to be known,
and cares not one bit
for approval;

who is this child
inside the man?
this soft masculine, lacking?

i am lessened by his weakness;
i am more for his innocence;
i am a mystery to myself,
in every regard;

would you read past sins
like so much gossip?

would you pore over pages
of failure, inadequacy?

would you settle into some
safe, voyeuristic un-life,
flipping from fellow to fellow
like channels on a flickering screen?

i have not chosen
this thin transparency;
no, it has chosen me.

Main and Merry

we were born here; reborn;
soil staining soles, grass
green, as tender roots
spread wide; rain, clean
as a newborn,
baptized soul;

beeswax burning
like smoldering hearts
at prayer;
beneath the sycamore leaves,
beside the stubble fields,
we skinned our knees
on lessons learned;
i would have held your hand,
if only i had known;

i can feel mother's kiss;
the waters of rebirth flowing
cool across my forehead;
the sting of soft correction;
the kiss of sacred wine
on virgin tongue;
the gentle dawn
of awe for my father's
humble ways;

the fragrant chrism glistening;
the purple wisps of pipe tobacco
soft-stepping the evening air;

not one of such things was lost;
all are now wrapped with care
in white tissue paper, held
in the bosom of remembrance;
laid-by for the days to come;
you keep such treasures, too;
i'm not the only one;

this door has creaked
and lurched beneath
the weight of ages,
since time out of mind;
nothing good ever fades;
and that which is gloriously broken
need never be fixed;

what comfort i find here,
amid the stones set
by builders come before;
stones i leapt - from then,
to now, to you;
the past was spent
to lead us here;
if only i had known;

what joy i now find
in your embrace,
that i'd have
held you then,
as i hold you now;
and much sooner
love would have
brought me home,
if only i had known;
if only i had known.

dad

dad loved the blackwater,
its cold belly dragged
over a carpet of woven
pine needles;
its shoulders sagging
beneath the weight of his canoe;

he loved to fish the lake
for bullhead -
scaleless, whiskered,
alarming in their primordial –
he laughed
when first i heard
the amphibious croak;

as i baited my hook,
he'd begin his
imperceptibly subtle
parenting, asking,

'so, what do you think?'
'about what?' i'd say;

and with ears, and heart, and mind wide open to each
beat of his little boy's heart, he'd reply with a smile,

'anything;'

and he always wanted to hear;
and he always wanted to know;

to learn; to love; to listen
far more than to speak,
far more than to assert;
and that's what he loved
about fishing, most;

he loved the slap
of the mallard's wings
against the soft
skin of the lake;

the white birch
parchment, rolled up
into scrolls;

the haunting 'who?'
of the ancient loon;
the timeless, worn,
and rounded peaks
of the mountains;

the carefree twang
of Roger Miller,
as much as
the dulcet tones
of Desmond, Brubeck,
Jobim, and Getz;

and the one thousand
and one nights
of Scheherazade;
he loved music,
and sweetly
(as was his way)
left it all to his children;

but most of all,
he loved mom;

and, loving her,
he loved his family;
and, loving us,
he loved
the generations to come;
the generations
who will also love
such things as:

fishing and listening;
and careful attention;
gentle fathering
of innocent souls;
excellent music;
the black water rippling
the breezy face
of Adirondack lakes
beneath mountains
older than
the bullhead,
and younger than
the loon;
loving more than
anything at all;
and letting love
define a life;

yes, dad loved many things,
and, oh, how he himself is loved.

pain

pain
is ubiquitous;

it sears body
and mind;

hiding
just below
appearance;

just behind
okay;

always dying
to be understood;

always questioning;
always pleading;
always wearing
its best and bravest;

i will inflict
no more;
i will add
not one
to its wretched sum;

suffering seeps
like blood
from a wounded heart;

every shattered hope,
every need unmet
weeps in secret,
crouches in shadows;
poisons the well
of all existence;

i will
staunch the flow;
i will
tread with care;
i will
sit with you,
in silence,
awhile;

injustice is the law
of the land; greed,
our sole inheritance;
fear, our solitary birthright;
confusion, our inevitable curse;
and over all is laid
insecurity,
the blanket
in which
we wrap
our cares;

i reject it utterly;
i take nothing
for myself;
i give what i am;
i will stand
and step aside,
that you might rise;

for we are
of a kind,
you and i;
and i besmirch
none but myself
with a lie;

and then...
in quiet vulnerability...

you shared your pain with me;
your quiet suffering,
your hidden hardships;
your fragments
of darkest agony;
the unfathomed
fracture in your soul;
your one remaining
wound, unshown;

and, in the sweet
economy of love,
your pain
became my own.

Oriole

in this sliver
of separation,
this fracture
of where,
we whisper
breathless
gazes in the breach;
touching only tips
of thankful wonder;

lengthened by unbroken,
timeless flecks of now
flow through pinched
glass, the tiniest hours
love might conceive;

you lament,
you can not
see me;
come, then,
and see;

you are at home
among the reeds;
the sighing mist;
the pulsing river;
the golden mink;
the new-brown beaver;
the prayerful turtles;

but you are more beautiful,
by far, than any
black-orange bird, elusive;
for you never do elude me;
you are always at my side;

parry the shapeless morn,
with shoulder-width rhythms
of one in and among
all that flows;

refresh your lungs
with this moment;
make it your own;
then, let it so become us;
that we, too, are one;
oh, how it does become us,
my love;

what i would not give
for three hours more;
to strip the scent of nature
from these lips;
to taste the sun-soaked
passion of wild meandering
along pathways wet
with listening;
to see, upon your hair,
these sunbeams
glistening.

A sunset viewed from behind

it's strange that,
being but one mile apart,
i feel close to you,
knowing...

we see the same moon;
we feel the same breeze;
we taste the same rain
from these clouds
we both see;

why is it that all we share
must be shared from afar?

such as when
you message me
to ask if the sunset
was rose and violet
and amber and gold
and fleeting and fading
and gone all too soon
when viewed from behind,
as it was from your room;

but i already knew,
for i spent the long evening
painting it for you.

broken bottles

broken bottles
overflowing with vacuous
disregard; this venomous
sludge corrodes
the virgin woods;

who knows
what fair creatures
endured?
who knows
what self-loathing
destroyed?

i cut my hand
on the dullard;
i puncture my feet
on the witless;
wretched seeps
into my grasping,
always striving
for innocence restored;

what have i gained this day?
with what have they parted?

i dig
beneath a layer of leaves -
even the forest covers herself
in modesty, wrapping
a shawl of shame

around her shoulders -
man sows only corruption;
we reap the earth we sow;

would that these bitter fruits
had soiled their lips;
would that these corpses
became them;

would that these ashes
could rise from the dead
and, with unsullied hands,
reclaim them.

Real poems

"but can you write
real poems?"

the child asked,
calling my life's
work into question;

casting aspersions
on the florid poetry of love;

tripping me flat on my
wounded pride;

"of course," i replied;

what else could i say?
while sinking into a soup
of self-questioning;

"try me!"

i was desperate, now,
to prove myself a poet
in every regard;

"make a pig poem!" he said;

"a poem about a pig?"

i clarified (though, in truth,

i was buying time);

"you're on!"

i cleared my throat,
the floor was mine:

"A pig
by any other name
is still a swine;"

"that's what i thought,"

he said,
and shook
his sweet head.

these hands

these hands
recall what the mind
relinquished to the moment;

if they trembled,
they trembled
in rhythm;
and what harmonies
sprung like youth
from soft fingertips,
like brilliance
from the mind
of a composer,
spoke nothing
before they met
your noble heart –
for every language
needs interpreting;
every note
must resound;

and in your hands
they moved a room
to silent awe;

one thought directing
each hand singly;

smoothing out the octaves,
beneath the white glare

of midday;

against the black gleam
of lacquered wood;

you led us, lost as you were
inside each excruciating
lilt; each deathly sigh;
each and every bleeding
drop of splendor;

you led us, along secret
pathways of poignant bliss;

and we all longed
to go with you,
and know the joys
of music
only you knew.

the world saps sweetness

the world saps sweetness
from our smiles;
leaving a shell of cynical;
a husk of distrust;

where understanding
takes effort, we doze
in drowsy apathy;
or spread the mire
of insecurity over
contemptuous weeds;

choosing always
the path of least
persistence,
we surrender to ease,
preferring distraction
to the harsh truths within;

are we so uncertain?
are we so tongue-tied?
that, lacking the power
to speak our ordered minds,
we wallow in weak emotion?

reason, a victim of feeling;
truth, a victim of desire;
and are we surprised
when the world
comes unhinged

and swings freely
in the winds
of howling indignation?

and what's to be done?
every wrong is one of injustice;
every slight, a selfish iniquity;
we search for reasons
to separate; classify,
organize, sort, and dismiss
along tribal lines, ensuring
our delicate hearts
and sleeping minds
never encounter
an idea too true,
a thought too foreign,
an individual too real;
vague people are safer
than solid persons;
none more solid than self;

it's true...
the world saps sweetness
from our smiles,
but sweetness can
smile back again,
the hearts and minds
of the world
to win.

clouds lead lives

clouds lead lives
of silent comprehension;
pondering the preponderance
of passing things below;

forming; drifting; fading;
their minds turned outward;
their hearts, pure gift;

like lumbering herds
of sage and subtle lambs,
they imbibe
the wisdom of the ages;
leaving only
dewdrop kisses
to moisten
languid cheeks;

there is no judgment
in their countenance;
no condemnation;
no reproach;

rather, wisps of gentle
smiling; tufts
of understanding;
as only hearts
who fathom such heights
could ever know;

if i had arms enough
to embrace them;

if i had tears enough
to cry;
i'd stand
in the shadow
of chaste compassion,
and never dare
to open
my eyes.

Carving space

from the curving
of the sunlight,
from the shapeless
of the air,
we carve out
a space around us
in which to touch;

fingertips, lips,
thoughts, and understanding,
weave our hearts together
with stitches of tenderness;

leaping back and forth
over healing seams -
me from you,
and you from me;

how could we move
amid the self-same starlight
and never once see
our shadows combine?

how did these flames
lose their warmth, but
that we could not embrace?

these days grow long;
and i cannot help
but see them

slip away;

each precious
press of palm to palm;
each calm caress
of moments
come and gone;
each meeting
of our eyes;
each laugh we share;
the thrill of stolen kisses
breathed through the evening air;

describe the folding of our lives,
a page turned; a chapter written
and sketched together;
even now,
lying here
with this poem,
i feel so much less
alone.

Waiting is over

...and, at last,
the waiting is over;
the distance contracts,
like elastic bands, released;
or magnets spun freely
across a level plane,
we collide in silent devastation;

a tender decimation of yearning;
a whispered release of souls
in wisps of exhalation;

like shades of mist and cloud
combining droplets
of me with you;

there is no time between us;
no passage of measured change;

only still, attentive, mindful
moments, indistinguishable
from eternal; inseparable
from each other; how did we
ever merit a love so pure?

...i pause from pondering,
and catch your eye –
for, somehow the evening
has passed us by.

Wadded balls of fluff

i have an idea, my love;
let me roll your ankle socks
into wadded balls of fluff;
like baby birds,
all feather and no substance,
that tumble from their nest
into clumsy flight;

then toss your socks
aside awhile;
and kissing each
by one
by ten
by all,
i'll add
my own collection
to this jumble
of bare caressing;
a merry gathering of funny,
fractured things; splintering
from the tapered ends
of limbs such as these;

then lead you by the hand;
your summer dress, a breeze
of cotton dreams, flowing
in subtle waves behind you
like joy follows
in your wake;
i'll kiss your fingertips,

each
by one
by ten
by all;

as we dance
among the dewfall;
and stain our bare feet
green with grass and laughter
and love and springtime;

until these twenty toes
are wrinkled with rain
and other youthful things;

then in the quiet
of the evening,
i'll wash the stains away
in soapy warmth
of bare caressing;
taking care to leave
memory untouched;
and kissing
each
by one
by all
by ten,
i'll hold
these toes
i love so well
and kiss
each
by all
again.

such tiny

such tiny
fingertips,
twirling strands
of you and me
into something
altogether us;

like pairs
of twisted wire,
we forge connections
through which surge
the free flow of life;

or, like ribbons running
down a horse's mane,
we tie together threads
of tenderness - weaving
chains to bind,
so beautifully,
these hearts;

if no man is an island,
then how much more
are we an archipelago?

a string of scattered
moments; a path of lily pads
upon which to dance
our days into evening;

do not be fooled
by gaps of separation;
by straights and narrows
through which wash
the wild tides
of daily life;
they are illusions;
for, we are not islands
in the sea;
but noble peaks
of an unbroken
mountain range
rising from the deep.

i went

i went
where the air
was clean and clear,
the better to see;

i walked
where the earth
was burdened
with much to say,
the better to listen;

i paused
where the land
was not my own,
in an effort to understand;

my own roots
have withered;
my own stalk is bent;
the old leaves
give no more shade;

perhaps, it is time
to open my eyes
to all that the wind
has, at my feet, lain,
and drink freely
of the summer rain.

This place

the sky
stood to its full height,
yawning with gaping grandeur;
arms stretched
high above its head,
fisted hands thrust
heavenward; exhaling
clouds of moldered vapor,
like scoops of vanilla
ice cream left to melt
on a marble slab;

but i, too small to reach
so far as heaven,
content myself
with the earth;

long leaves cutting limbs
(licking sweaty salt-wounds)
sting the itchy summertime;
i drown in gulps of green,
beneath the blue of waterless;

sending ripples out in all
directions; swimming
through thickening grain;

i plow the hedgerow
with my feet, and trample
tender weeds like Medea's

young; until, at last, i am lost
(knowing only up and down);

the infinite blue ether,
and the serrated
tongues of deaf corn;
mine, the only ears in the field;
mine, the only feet free to roam;

to think, that i once
called this place my home;
among the whispering
stalks, one is never alone.

Memorial Day

how inadequate to the task
is the bracketing of a life
between two dates;

two breaths, the first,
the last; what of the end
was present at the start?
and how unlike beginnings
our endings are;

each marker, a feeble grasp
at eternal; three generations
worth of remembrance, at best,
until the earth herself
sinks beneath the weight
of crumbling mortality;

how uneven these garden
paths; how weather-worn
these stones; how moving
the trinkets of affection
left behind by the living;

but here lies one, in glory
enshrined; the dates of his
service and final oblation;
how such selfless acts of love
do enrich the soil of a nation.

Day of Memoriam

among the tombstones,
i walked in silent contemplation,
and listened to the wisdom
of a century of trees;

the breeze, her quilted arm
wrapped round my shoulder,
guiding me along paths
i had not trodden in decades;

names and dates, etched
in the scaly, peeling faces
of once-eternal stone;

"In the year of Our Lord,"
"United above," "Thou"
and "Thine" and other
outlived phrases, all fallen
from usage as the world's
heart hardened -
turning inward, always inward;

but is that not the definition
of the damned? i find none here;
i daren't, lest it, one day, be me;

pausing, i take my place
among the dead, sitting
in a shady patch of green;
running my hands through strands

of the earth's own weaving,
like lines from a tactile poem
of spring, summer, autumn -
let me be buried in winter;
the season of my birth, a deliberate
end to an unplanned start;
the season of my great love,
the destiny of a shattered heart;

and i wondered, what does it mean
to live? to die? to be remembered
wrongly, always wrongly,
despite a generous epitaph;

but is this not the definition
of living? i find none here;
only a fragment of stone,
and the assurance that lives,
though brimming o'er
with meaning,
need not be well known.

mom

my mother
knew mostly jealousy;
(poor soul, she was flawed,
just like me)
my father's love
was her greedy
treasure; and this was,
beyond a doubt,
understandable;
for it would surely
have been
to anyone he loved
so much as my mother;

in the smallest recesses
of her insecurities,
she could endure no rival,
not strangers, nor phantoms,
nor daughters, nor not-quite-friends,
only God - to her, synonymous,
with Dad, and therefore quite safe;

she never learned
life's elusive lessons:
to cradle happiness in the heart;
to cultivate joy from the menial;
to give thanks for the tiny allotments
from life's daily stores;

i do not blame her;

as it surely must be
for my own kids
through me,
it was only through her fractures
that i was able to see
that which she never could:

how to smile,
and laugh,
and love
someone utterly
other than self;

and across my own modest,
restrained laughter,
a shadow of disapproval
still lies;

she loved me,
she knew she should;
and i her, as was natural -
without question or thought
or overly-much affection,
as was her generation's way -
the heart fared worse than children,
neither seen nor heard;
(poor dysfunctional thing,
a generation flawed,
just like me);

then, in an instant, i matured
beyond myself: i was not
the center of her world;
she existed before me,
as fully formed

and utterly other
as if she were not
(imagine it)
contingent upon me,
as i am upon her;

it was then
that i set aside the child
and, jealous of my youth,
mourned to be a man;

as she aged into shadows,
trifles and affectations
fell away,
being but baggage
of the mind -
and that, too, fell away,
like so many blossoms
on a late autumn day;

what was left
was true,
the brain being
but a crumb;
a lonely stranger;
a vaporous phantom;
a morsel of Mom;
lacking everything
that was not her;
and what remained
was a smile
and the innocent
love of a child.

some there are

some there are
who love this land;
whose blood
is a thick mud
of loam and compost;
whose lungs exhale
the husks of wheat;
whose cracked skin
is mortared with manure,
a laboursome mosaic
of pastoral stained glass;

some there are
whose hearts beat
with the raw rhythms
of the earth;
who sense the seasons change
before ever a tender bud is born
or a stem lets fall the dying leaf;
who breathe the same air
as all things living,
and till the soil
made fertile by the blood
of those who tilled before;

some there are
who live and die, unsung,
as silent as seasons decline.

Silk rose

this...

token of reluctant parting;
promise of swift return;
reminder of how we started,
of childhood grown
beyond all words;

our sweet forget-me-not flower;
our first-ever winter bloom;
the sigh of wordless poems;
the kiss of a skylight moon;

the blush of one snowy evening;
an unspoken vow in the night;
a symbol of utmost meaning;
assurance of all that is right;

...this, my love,
this, our simple
silk rose.

like kittens

like kittens
of sugar-white
and idle-orange,

all tangled
in raveled balls
of red string, knotted,

we are *glee-ridden*,
my love;

(the phrase is your own,
as i and my heart and soul
shall remain);

we groom
the matted
mops
        of this
                and that
                        and every
                mess
        ever
scattered
in the kennels
of our hearts;

locks and bars
and mesh
through which

to watch
the world;

was happiness ever
the runt of longing?

had we but known
it is the child of woe,
then...
troubles,
once come,
might all the
sooner
go.

these buds stand silent

these buds stand silent
in the summer sun;
like votive lights
in a sanctuary of prayer,
they echo love and pleading:

> "remember, dear one, remember
> all that we have meant;
> all that we once were;
> all that we've become;
> remember what awaits,
> and the flickering of our colors,
> the bowing of our petaled
> heads will not have been in vain;"

if i could press
each blossom to my lips,
i would deliver them all
to your soft cheek;

if i could conceal myself
behind each scent,
the spirit of my essence
hidden in the unclad air,
i might whisper
in your ear while you sleep:

> "i love you, and there has
> never been a love so deep."

July 4th, 1972

in the light
of a quarter moon,
beneath the burst
of colored stars,
the very night
this nation was born,
on a cool summer's eve,
our parents did conceive
us both, not two miles apart;

is this not
how soulmates
are made?
is this not
what our prayers
would have prayed?

to be exhaled
into existence
as one divine sigh;

for there never
was a me
apart from you;

and i never
knew a world
you never knew;

and, in that fire

of passion
most pure,
after God
had left His mark
upon your heart,
He deigned
to leave the same
upon my own;

twin flames kindled
from the self-same spark;

one mind, one soul,
one spirit formed,
then gently drawn apart;
how gently drawn apart;

still, i have
ever been thine,
yes, even from
our start.

beyond hope

beyond hope;
beyond expectation;
beyond all reason;

you are here
by my side;

fitting snuggly
into the spaces
of my life, as i,
in yours, abide;

arms entwined,
embracing those
we love,
as sweetly
as if divinely
preordained;

we sit and sort
the hope chests
of our hearts:

these memories, yours;
these memories, mine;
so many photographs
in which we both
appeared - ever
close, and ever
drawing near;

how softly
do the hours
transform themselves
to days, and months
become the milestones
of our lives, and memories
forged enrich
our waning years;

but is this not
why you and i are here?

to live, to love, to give
of who we are?

to cultivate
these fortunate
hearts, making
of our lives
a living
work of
art.

Shooting star

i saw the night sky split;
a finger, chapped,
drawn slowly over a bolt
of black silk,
sparked a firestorm
of gaping wonder;

i am not, yet, too old
to mark the magic
in the heavens;

no, this night, i grew
young in the twinkling
of a star;

my cold, aching heart
felt its warmth a while;

my splintered mind,
its solitary resolve;

my fumbling words were
but a folly of description;

why does beauty often
run its course too soon?
why are some stars doomed
to fall only in the afternoon?

perhaps, it was enough

that i was there
to mark this silent death;
to feel its tears
of starlight stain my face;
to inhale its fair
and final breath;

for i, like she, pass
unnoticed through the night;
when so much of this life is lived
concealed from others' sight.

is it any wonder

is it any wonder
that i love you?

behold your noble spirit;
the innocence of your heart;

how fluently the incorporeal
essence of your soul utters
grace and goodness to my mind;

how effortlessly your body renders
all that beauty might define;

you are she; ever ancient,
ever new; poised upon
a pedestal of feminine genius;

strength without conquest;
reach without grasp;
taking upon yourself
the form majestic;
humbly reflecting the heavens
to mere mortals below;

this pose triumphal
is the triumph of our race;
and in the modest shadows,
i know and love your face.

A lover's tale

when the second hand slowed,
sweeping the silent clock face
bare; easing, subsiding, abating,
pulsing no more;
all became profound stillness...
and my world ceased to be.

i drew the dank darkness
of solitude and loathe
reluctance around
my shoulders; i pulled
the bleak empty of pointless
across my bowed and broken back;

and then i settled-in to die...
death being all, and i being
nothing much at all;

i felt it fitting to decay;
i thought it wisdom to wither;
thinking not that you
would seek me out
from among the warped
wreckage of my life;

but how i love you for this,
and that, and the other
many things which denote you truly;
like the graceful strength
of your skillful dancer's legs;

the elegance of your subtle limbs;
the poise of your all and every;
the cosmic of our embrace;
the spiritual of our union;
the boundless of your smiling lips;
the softness of your every inch;
the beauty of - dear God,
but you are Anguish, herself;

you gently bruise my weakness;
you lovingly injure my frailty;
you wonderfully wound my insufficiency;
until, nothing remains but
that which loves you;
for, i do love you,
and what is more than this?

i am a stream of consciousness,
trickling tediously, spilling fruitlessly
my every drop - word by tortured word -
into the basin of your throbbing sea;

i am a wisp of mindfulness,
distracted by the way your laughter
conjures wildflower meadows,
forgotten memories, and
timeless, tender kisses to my mind;

i am an unspent kindness,
nothing more, and nothing
more useless than this;
awaiting that which calls
my love to action: You;

the latent flawlessness of You;

the agile thoughtfulness of You;
drawing life from lifeless;
drawing love from heartless;
drawing all my dreams indelible;

beyond all expectation,
the second hand has sprung
again to life:
promising love for love,
and you for me,
and vows for man and wife.

what good are words?

what good are words?
these tools of my trade,
what value do they possess?

they stutter similes;
they mutter metaphors;
they do not sing the heart;

they can but speak the mind,
and that, done poorly;

for, what is the mind,
but a collection
of certain confusion;
a disarray
of fickle convictions;
an organ, limp and languid,
occupying space,
and owing rent in arrears;

i am done with thinking;
it profits me nothing;

thoughts are but frail arguments
forged to undermine assurance;

i blush at their ignobility,
ashamed of their duplicity;

but, soft...

be still...

for, i see you there,
seated, as you are,
upon the throne of my heart;

and all words fade to useless;
all thoughts resolve to one:

you are she...

my God, but these
three words
are sweet:

you
are
she...

i know you of old;
has there ever been a moment
when you were not there?

was there ever a day
when we were apart?

in 18 years,
could we have been
more present
one to the other?

and did not the intervening
paths wind
among hills,
and valleys,

and blinds,
and broad vistas
of slow recognition,

until...

you are she...

and, i,
to you,
i am he...

and, oh,
how i love thee
in words
and wordlessly.

Awaiting

we stand upon a threshold;
your hand in mine, waiting;
breathless as the doldrums
in July; our eyes fixed
upon Our Mother's face;

expectant, certain of the outcome,
the decree that will set us free;
for i am bound, like you,
as tethered, as i am, to thee;

what are these patient days?
what lessons do they teach?
but to love, and never forget
that this was not
of our own making;

look back over the years,
each month of our lives -
i was there; you were there;
even in the hours of separation,
we did but wander in the dark,
certain of the fact that,
what the heart desires,
must surely exist; anything less
would be a cruel and spiteful ruse;

my love, you overwhelm me;
this mind cannot contain
what my heart

writhes to hold;
you are too much you
for too little me;
you are grace poised
upon the petal of a rose;

you are the blush
of morning; the reflection
of evening; the nuanced
repose of subtle night;
you are flawless beauty
too bright to behold;
you are modesty
too fragile to hold;

you are the full summation
of my every unspoken desire;
and every urge within me
yearns to speak your name;
every corner of my soul
longs to grapple itself
to you with rings
of silver-gold;

and so we wait;
balanced on the edge of faith;
behind us, the past,
with all its twisted paths;
before us, a life,
by love made straight.

let me spend my days

let me spend my days,
ink-stained and heart-sleeved,
penning poems of frustrated
description; writing words
of dire yearning, longing
just to sketch the fair outlines
of your slightest touch;

those fingertips which,
with delicate precision,
unfold the flower of my soul;

those eyes whose limitless
waters draw me - darker
by deeper, by mislaid -
into wells of wistful wandering;

those lips which speak both
wisdom and kisses -
for, are they not the same?

to cleave the very heart of me;
let me thus spend all my days;

but, in the evening,
when the chalky sky runs
wet with streams of pastel
reverence, let me read
my works of passion to you;

each syllable, a raindrop;
each sentiment, a seedling;
each poem, a promise made,
to love you ever more perfectly
by each, by every day.

there is grace

there is grace
in serendipity;
there is order
behind the chaos;

i would rather cast myself
to the four winds
of providence
than live an un-life
rooted to the ground;
safe but sorry;
predictably sterile;

watching the world
through a tiny pale screen
flickering distraction,
while sunsets
pass unseen;

come, take my hand,
let us dance
among the raindrops;
splash, barefoot and childlike,
through the puddles;
take off our clothes
and run naked
through the summer evenings
of our slowly-aging youth;

that we might kiss

the lightning
bugs; lie in the tall grass
and let the bunnies pad
velvet cottontails down
our bare backs;

let laughter tickle our toes
and giggle in our smiles,
until all that remains
are dimples, and memories,
and you, and me, and
one last kiss
beneath the willow tree.

Bald Mountain

gnarled knuckles
of arthritic stone
clutch roots,
weathered
and worn
by too much
striving;

the wrinkled mountain
bows his tonsured head,
his back bent
beneath the weight
of ages past
and the prospect
of countless more
to come;

soaking the soreness
from his feet
in lakes stained
brown by decaying
tannins - tea left slowly
to steep for an age
of the earth -
his muddy toes
tangle among
the shadows
of secret grasses;

all mysteries lie

open to the wind;
but what lay hidden
in the deep, only
bedrock can tell;

jutting from precarious,
clinging to perilous,
trees bind their fortunes
to slopes of tumbling
decline;

the dimpled earth
grinds through
frictions of gravel;
slowing, slipping, listing,
heaving-over to plunge
through the echoless abyss;
even then, will this mountain
remain, until gnawed
and swallowed up
by bitter rains.

i love that you are

i love that you are;

that you breathe in
scented whispers;
that you breathe out
sated sighs;

that you ever
were before me,
that i might be
forever yours;

(forever
has been
flourishing
in us
ever more
and
ever more)

i love
that i can
see you;

i love
that you are
real;

i love it when
you touch me

as if i were
flesh and bone,
and not just he
whom you once knew
by name,
when, once,
we lived alone;

i love
the many ways
you find to be
the truest you;
and all
the truest love
behind each loving
thing you do.

Mornings of middle age

what an eclectic composite
is middle age; not unlike
me as a teen
having outgrown
insecurity; voice cracks;
and acne;

then, i was a child
longing to be a man;
now, i am a man
musing on the
moments of my youth;

i start my day
with prayer,
aligning myself
to a Greater Reality,
reminding myself
of my place
amid the wonders
of creation;

i am content
to be but a crumb
of meaning, and nothing
more; it is enough
to be what one truly is;
and a blessing
beyond worth
to know;

having strengthened
the spirit,
i then subject
the body; i run
to outpace death;
i lift to harden
resolve; i paddle
to find my way;

and always
the body asks, "why?"
poor, poor, plaintive child,
will you never embrace
more than you are? alas;

now comes that
for which my soul was made:
the fruitless pursuits
of heart and mind;
i have ever been
impractical;

on my desk sit
four books:
CS Lewis, Louise Glück,
Mary Oliver,
and (the most unlikely)
US Army Survival Manual;

in these morning devotions,
i explore God, cynicism,
wonderment, and endurance -
and confess to understand
less and less, the more i try;

as i sip my cold coffee,
reading,
letting the words pass
through me like ghosts
on a foggy afternoon,
i feel them condense
like raindrops on the sinuous
fibers of my inner clockwork,
oiling the gears of my heart,
by which i measure
this latest age of my life;
by which i strive
to see and always
choose the right.

barefoot and wistful

grasping desperate
hands full of coarse,
green hair,
like the mane
of a muddy horse
upon whom i rest
all my hopes, and dreams,
and memories,
and moments past;

the ground sweats
beneath me,
laboring as she does
ever to give me birth;

i am no less her child,
though least
among her children, i am;

i bury my face
where, one brief day,
the rest shall follow;

inhaling dark odors
of decay; i see the efforts
of the hidden mole,
blindly reacting
to obstacles in his way,
like me, and so like me;

swimming in a sea
of ether, carving broad
swathes of sky
in arcs of effortless,
two hawks glide
upon motionless wings;

i love them,
for they make
my love smile
as, down below
in the grass,
we sit, barefoot
and wistful,
for a while.

into the darkness

into the darkness;
down stone-lined pathways,
closer than daylight,
closing in;

with echoing footsteps
of unseen names
so many of whom
we both knew;

beneath a veil of thin
and ghostly aspect,
i held your hand
for comfort;

(is not every
true meaning
really only *love*?)

silhouettes and shadows
leap into our minds;
crouching like panthers;
soft, padded paws of fears
we cannot control;

instead,
let us go out
to meet them,
these specters,
these ticks,

and spiders,
stinging bees,
and stranger things
than we dare speak
of in daylight;

if one night of discomfort
can bring courage
to your mind,
then this life i live
will not have been
simply mine.

whenever you're gone

sitting here with you
miles away
is like splaying wide
the vulnerable marrow
to flaying fingers
of scraping, etching,
teasing my senses
free from the fibers
of my soul; adrift
on a dark, silent sea;
no sight but inner gazing;
a kind of madness
of the heart;

alone is an emptiness
i can describe
only in peculiar,
wordless groans;
who would listen?
who would know?

is this hand
not a curious thing?
it holds nothing
so well as your own;
and grasps only hope
whenever you're gone.

what of me

what of me
is allowed
to keep
the
this
and
that
of unkept
possessions?

when i
cannot
even keep
this body
beyond
death's
register;

i carry
no receipt;
no proof
of ownership;
no certificate,
but that of
birth;

what of me
or in me
is just me?
just

and only
me?

that he might
file a claim?

that he might
place demands
against a warranty
voided by
recklessness;

for there
is nothing
more reckless
than life
fully lived,
nothing
except
for
love;
nothing
except
for
l
o
v
e
.

there is an infinite number

there is an infinite number
of things i will never be;
for i am bounded by finite;
tangled in time;
mired in thick,
slogging space;

inertia grasps my heels
in both hands,
jealous as she is
of fleet momentum,
shackling me earthbound,
when i might
rather scale
the ragged walls
of mortality
and cast myself
headlong into adventures
unknown;

these foes
must i contend with;
these foes
and many more;

crouching in the corners
of my mind,
hidden in the weeds
that grow to seed,
fear and insecurity

sap lifeblood
at its source;
doubt whispers poison
into every susceptible,
rendering stillborn
all the offspring
of invention;

even at its best,
impatience yearns
to close the distance
between effort and result,
imperiling the task at hand;
endangering all becoming;
rotting to ruin
the tender buds
of spring;

seething with discontent
at the prospect of mastering
but one,
ambition casts
too wide a net,
sputtering effort
like so much spittle;
hauling at the ropes
to land an empty take;

then, in truth,
if infinite
i can never be,
then let me
find contentment
in finite me.

father

this same air once billowed
your lungs, thin; brown,
paper sacks crumpled
and wadded with age;

i hear their crinkling wheeze,
like baffles of membrane;
fluttering life in lessening
efforts of defeat, you acquiesce;

if i could sift the silted dirt
to powder, i might just find
one tiny eyelash of yours -
some thirty years old -
from when you used to live
and lived that life-lived here;

before the ruin it (and you, and i)
became; Father, did you ever think
we'd both be here
where we find ourselves now?

you, in the cold earth;
i, making sense of old ground;

the tireless turning
of the seasons,
churns something
to nothing;
treading underfoot

every lash and limb,
and nail clipping,
until all that remains
are all those remains
and this same air
that once billowed
your lungs, thin;

inhaling, i hold you
near, knowing, as i do,
that you must surely
leave me again.

if i could learn to listen

if i could learn to listen,
then might i utter wisdom;

if i could train my ear,
then might i restrain my tongue;

if i could open my mind,
then might i shut out all folly;

for, the smaller i am
the less i might hold;

if i had the courage to feel,
then might i show compassion;

if i could fathom my guilt,
then might i share forgiveness;

if i could see without judgement,
then might i taste truth's sweetness;

for, the world is a palette of infinite hues;
and i, but a painting child at play;

if, before my end has come,
if, in you, i can learn to love,
then might we make
the world anew;

one heart, one mind,

one kindly smile;
one patient pause
to give attention for awhile;

we would not fear
the chaos of descending gloom,
for, the darker the night
the greater the brightness
of one small light.

blush, envious sky

blush, envious sky;
your moments slip
suddenly into forgotten;

your now
never was;
your was
cannot linger
beyond the reach
of far distant horizons;

i lay stricken
at the feet
of one more glorious
than you; though your
brushstrokes smooth –

layer by whisper by
scent of fair longing –

broad remembrance
in a million subtle
tones, nighttime
threatens
to swallow
you whole;

what promise
could you make
that i might believe?

there is no time left
in this day
to honor vows;

you are a passing thing,
but one
in a world
of passing things;
my love, alone,
remains;

blush, envious sky;
what more can you do,
than lend the striated earth
the contrast of your light?

one last kiss,
before we surrender
to the night.

we are all broken

we are all broken;
each one of us,
healing, questioning,
faltering beneath
our birthright;

shifting the weight
of our human condition
from this shoulder
to that; each of us
hoping desperately;
despairing hopelessly;

sinking beyond the reach
of ourselves; hiding
just beyond touch
of one another;

posturing to compensate
for that which
we cannot find
when searching
for ourselves;

sifting through the scraps
of other's words
and nuances
for any semblance
of self; fearful
of turning our eyes

inward; trying
always to drown
the whispers
of our hearts
in the din
of distraction;

oh, if only
we could silence
the cacophony
of falsehoods,
we might
know the glory
of being
damaged goods.

this momentary wisp

this space
is familiar to me;
this voice,
echoing off soft walls
of sinew and flesh,
has always been
my own;

this frame
of calcified timbers,
creaks beneath the burdensome
cares of dwindling days;

i am replaced,
cell by ruptured cell;
i am renewed;
passing silently
into death,
holding fast
to tenuous life;
the handoff accomplished
without fumbling
the blood red baton;

who am i,
that i was not yesterday?
who am i,
that i will not be tomorrow?
who am i,
but that which i am today?

no more; no more;

for, to be
at all
is to be
all at once
today;

these muscles harden
in the ache of usage;
wither in a moment
of neglect; i have become
a diminishing return;

when use erodes ability,
and disuse atrophies,
what choice have i
but to surrender
to grave mortality?

beneath my jawbone,
a flutter in the neck -
how strange to lay
my fingers upon
the stumbling
of my own heart;

why suffer so,
if all gains be temporary?
save those of becoming...
those of achievement...
those of remembrance...
and the noble pursuit
of inspiring self

and others
to live;

for all life
is a gift;

and i am
who i am -
this
momentary
wisp.

you are so easy to love

you are so easy to love;
in wordless
and spoken,
you hear
what my heart contains;

each effort
finds fulfillment;
each silence
finds its rest;

all i have to give
becomes so seamlessly
yours; as all you gracefully are
so beautifully becomes you,
that i might better be
thine, and being thine
become more truly me;

oh, that i never knew
myself, until i learned
to see through your eyes;

oh, let me never forget
gratitude; and, overwhelmed
by awareness, by mindful
moments of peaceful pause,
let me turn myself to you
until only Us remains;

how well designed
is love,
that, in seeking first
your joy, my own is secured;

that, in emptying myself
of self,
i might embrace
much more of you;

that, in all this weary world,
you are;

a miracle
i could never understand:

two hearts
from one flame, divine;
that i was made
to be yours,
and you were made
to be mine.

do not hide the scars

do not hide the scars,
the wounds, the pain,
the myriad stains
of tears etched deep
beneath the surface
of a smile held
tenuously in place;

there is shame
only in deception,
only in denial
of yourself
and the ubiquity
of suffering;

to be human
is to hurt; there
is no other way;

each bruise you bear
is proof positive;
the truest, most irrefutable
certificate of your birth;

your irrevocable enrollment
in the human race,
to which your life
adds the elegant
adornment of
unrepeatable you;

a mosaic of lights
and darks; the stained
glass luminosity of
a beauty composed
of each and every
excruciating fact
of the forging
of your soul;

why would you hide?

consider what you conceal:

if each fractured fragment
is but a facet of you,
what would remain?
what would be true?
and who would you be
apart from all these wounds?

things belong

things belong
to us;
various and sundry;
stuff and bothersome;
items left to languish
in a lost and found;

for, what does it mean
to belong?

but to always
be longing?

a fussy absorption;
a troubled disquiet
over moth and moldering;

ever-brooding in anxious
concern; overly solicitous
to possess over-much;

excessive in uselessness;
wasted on wanton;
squandering all precious;

losing but little
and counting it great loss;

much by more by many
by imperceptibly shrinking,

we are consumed
with consumption;

our lives retold in retail;
bought and sold
without receipt;

no returns; no refunds
on hopes and dreams
and lives and loves all lost;

only a blackhole of accretion
of much by more by many
by imperceptibly empty;

wanting, by declension, then,
to own other souls;
other creatures;
other peoples;

for, i am
the center of this hole;

and i want, i want,
i am what i want;

never
what i say; what i do;
what i give; what i think;

what i want
has become
all that i love;
all that i live;
but...

no more!

i say,
no more!
no more!

for, true wealth
is in being;
in becoming;
and in loving;

to make room
for these
longings-to-be,
i want
no more
belongings
for me.

this Us we build

this Us we build;
in depth of feel;
by knowing,
connecting;
upon solid piers
of esteem,
we spiral upward;
admiring the grandeur
of a soul;
traveling apace,
down paths
of astonished,
we know
what it is
that we've found;

the more these meanings
discover, the more words
fail to say; for, we have
spoken more eloquence
before; with silent lips
caressing
silent lips (caressing),
we leave
no space
for any
but certainty;

beneath this calm
flow of serene,

impatient currents
churn; rending rill
from bedrock
and longing from
yearning; it is not
for reaching
that i have grown
restive; but for holding
you ever-near;

with the last,
dying breath of spoken,
i will end all words
with true;
and profess my vow,
unbroken,
that i shall
forever and always
love you.

tattoos

there are tattoos, hidden
beneath the fibers
of this shirt; meaning,
seared like needlepoint
into receptive skin;
hot blood through veins
coursing black ink; pain
enshrined; inscribed in living flesh,
milestones of deep identity
depict my inward, outwardly;
i have become a non sequitur,
a paradox of scandalous sketches;
jolting others from prejudice;
subverting expectations;
smashing stereotypes,
like so many small, fragile
minds; confusing assumptions,
worlds collide in creative
big bangs of elegant rebirth;
God forbid i ever slip
into predictable, fall
into convention, or sell
my soul for safe and same;
let me, rather, tear the veil
of conformity apart,
and make of this life
a work of art.

life is a lengthening

life is a lengthening
of memories lost;
moments strained
by remembrance;
impressions, little more;

in wisdom, i look back
on foolish youth, still longing
for such freedom as ignorance
affords; if i had known then,
i would not now be who i am;

whirling like a winsome cyclone
of impatient demands,
i rend time from each passing now;

draining color from the pale face
of day, until lifeless stretches out
behind me in vast, littered fields
of forgotten; such was my state,
when you found me;

such is my state,
when we're apart;

and i ask myself,
if i had endless lives to live,
how would i live each one?

with you; infinite moments;

with you; wasting no time;
with you; regretting nothing;
with you; living, loving, exploring;

becoming so much more
with you; and marking time
would cease to be
a melancholy chore
with you at my side,
even now and evermore.

flesh stiffens, hardens

flesh stiffens, hardens
in the thin, cracked
shell of morning;

the air itself falls
shattered on the ground
at my feet, the hopes
of a winter's day;

all is blue, and that
which could not bear it,
contracts in wrinkles
of white woe;

death never looked so tragic,
so harsh, so unforgiving
as she does beneath the stagnant
suggestion of sunlight,
it enlivens nothing,
not even the smallest something;

for, as surely as winter follows fall,
there is, in me, no warmth i can recall.

in all the selfless ways

in all the selfless ways,
i love you;

but do not, my love,
begrudge me
the selfish ways, too;

i would not waste
a single mode
of touching you,

life being short,
and me being thine,
and love being all we need;

oh, but, i would have you,
as the earth possesses
the moon; for, you shine
on me and i brashly
call you my own;

is your brilliance
that you deign to shine
at all? or that you smile
upon a lesser such as i?

in all the yesterways,
i know you;

in all forever ways,

i will be true;
for, every stumble
learns agility;

not every trip
becomes a fall;

in loving you
i come myself to know;

how very like selfless
this, my, selfish grows.

life lived fully

life lived fully:
eschewing sadness,
unhappiness set aside;
joy at arm's length,
grasping tangential;
touching all; reaching
beyond stifling self
to connect with other,
more other, ever only other;

bathing wild
in floods of meaning;
hearing wonder
where common speaks;
creating adventure,
when waiting wastes
precious, irretrievable; and
not yet belies the moment;

recklessly loving; willingly
trusting; humbly forgiving;
surrendering self
for the sake of belief
that life is worth living
and time, all too brief.

Reflections on the 90-Miler

this place regards me
not at all; i do not
so much as tickle
the tendrils
of the mountain,
my feet being
but dust and ash;

he is no grandfatherly spirit;
he is no god; he stands aloof,
indifferent to all
but the slow rise
and timeless crumbling
of his own petrous heart;

this mountain has lived
too long, and forgotten
all ancient kindness;

who speaks like the river?
who whispers, 'follow me'
and i am fool enough to go;

beneath the glassy eye
of her watery visage,
strands of auburn locks
flow like vacant ghosts
of spectral vapor;

and i am mesmerized

by the swaying
of her tireless hips,
carrying me unwittingly
to my doom;

these lakes are nothing
more than shards
of shattered mirrors
on the floor; held
in the hands of the hills,
who have only
to spread their fingers
and all is lost; i feel them tease
with cruel condescension;

this long lake denies me
any milestone, any marker
by which to mete out the monotony;
without change, hope dies
beneath the blistering sun;

i thirst;
are these not
the Savior's own words?
a solitary mast
in a sea of souls,
and none to give Him comfort;

my Lord, I know your plight;
for, surrounded by water,
i dare not drink;
in place of gall,
i taste only spite.

run the hidden paths

run the hidden paths
of the world with me,
barefoot and giggling;
let us always be young;

see the seamless raiment
of the sky, the hand-stitched sun,
the quilted clouds of pillowy
vastness; all as unbroken
as the world's first morn;

lay beneath this child's
blanket, this tent of bedtime
wondering; we raise our hands
to pull the pinpricked sky
of star-speckled, moon-drops,
and silken softness over our heads;

cuddle close to me, your cheek
against my own;
share this breath,
this warmth, these hues
of color cast by rainbows;

swim this sea of green,
these waves of bladed grass;
circling stems and petals
in our way; let me kiss your
fingertips, wrinkled by the dew;

lick the morning from our lips;
dive deep beneath the undulating
earth, reclaiming youth and innocence
from the womb of our birth;

let us grow young together;
let us be crippled by joy;
let us lose our lives to each other;
let us die of foolhardy love;
timeless, ageless as we are;

these ghosts which haunt
the hallways of flesh and bone,
they're free, unfettered, unbound
by clocks unwinding;

for, what is time?
but days and months and years
since you were mine?

there is not enough, here

there is not enough, here;
not enough hope;
not enough worth;
not enough summer,
warmth or sunlight
to give joy to each birth;

too little laughter;
and too few smiles;
not enough time
to sit and speak
for a while;

but there is
plenty of sadness;
and plenty of grief;
plenty of nothing;
and no hope of relief;

too much dependence;
and too much despair;
too many lies, many whys,
everywhere;

too little heart,
and too little soul;
and too few who care,
of the too few who know.

i love the whats

i love the whats
and hows of you,
the wheres
that you
once knew;

and as i learn
the many whys,
i love your
reasons, too.

we are hope

we are hope;
we are faith
confirmed;

we are
each other's
reason to believe;

ours is the smile
that changes
all things;

ours, the hands
that raise up;

ours, the ear
that listens;

ours, the heart
that understands;

ours are the eyes
that soften with care;

and the feet that hasten
to give aid in need;

we must ever freely give,
as we freely receive;

and never shy away
from the perils
of sympathy;

the dangers
of compassion;

the madness
of love;

know this,
and never waver
in your belief:

that nations change,
not by decree or law
or conquest of arms,

but with the gentle
turning of each heart,

by the silent whisper
of a smile,

in countless
hidden trivialities
of kindness;

for nothing good
is ever lost

in the serendipitous
grace when two paths cross.

if i could look in

if i could look in
upon your sleeping,
downy-draped heart;

the face of innocence
padded upon privileged pillows;
enviable, they rest themselves
against your cheek;

like quilted clouds
of seamless stitching,
you breathe silence
to my longing;

eyes closed, heart open,
you draw me ever deeper -
for yours is a heart
unlike any i've known:

birdsong and wistful,
a diamond solitaire
in a box fretted
with silver
and moonbeams -
i would but love you
more;

if i could run drowsy
streaks of watercolor
down your darkened windowpane,

and stain your sill
in pastels of tenderness,
would you wake
in the morning
to know i was there?

would you gather me up,
like autumn leaves
amid drooping summer
blades of green and yearning;

hold me like a keepsake;
arrange me in right order?

for upon each leaf,
i have written one line
in a poem to your heart;

i wonder,
would you love me
more?

if i could wrest
these moments
from the indifferent
grasp of time,
i'd gladly sell myself
as ransom to the night –

to buy back every second
i have lost to slumber,
just to sleep them anew
at your sweet side.

these clouds draw my eye

these clouds draw my eye,
pearl inlay on Wedgwood,
unglazed porcelain
of powder blue;

they spread themselves
against the setting sun,
translucent to its gaze,
their thin cotton fringe
clouding hearts
of flannel grey;

oh, that i might
sink my toes
into their winter dreams;

that i might
wrap my shoulders
in their kindness,
and watch in wide wonder
as warm, wandering sunbeams
weave a path between
the frost and my frigid sighs;

see how the shadows fall
in deep contrast
and cold opposition;

cautious, they lead
the eye of the beholder

away, away, always away;

they have no purpose,
but to lie in light's leeward;

heel to heel, a pale imitation
of real; a ghost in the meadow;
the darker side of sunset;

the eggshell sky is chipped,
and, somewhere
among the hills,
a curved and concave
fleck of fragile
lay rocking
in the restless breeze;

a window upon
what grace has sown:
the sacred glow
of God's own throne.

the sky opens her arms

the sky opens her arms
of blue droplet gossamer,
drawing sunrise to her breast,
like a weary child;

i am too small to notice,
too fleeting to take seriously;

she has seen my sort before,
for, we sprout and wither
like glorious weeds, beneath
her indifferent eye;

what am i ,
that you should ask my name?
i am not the sky; i am dust and
forgetful, ink-stained fingers
fretting over choice of words;

clouds bear me up on backs,
smooth, pale, and naked;
and i wonder if i tickle
their doughy rolls of muffin tops;

what was it that once set me
wandering? seeking?
what was it i hoped to find?
i never knew, until i found you;

did i spread the wispy folds

of ephemeral, to search you
hidden there? did i lick the moisture
of a thousand sunsets from my lips,
thinking to taste your spirit?

the sky conceals no wonders
for me, now; no more;
i have seen her sort before;

she is not you; she is too small
to notice, too blue to comprehend;
too unlike my love, my soulmate,
to ever again be my friend.

red earth

red earth,
i know you;
your iron dust odor
coats my nostrils
like crusted blood;

i taste the sweetness
of pulverized quartz;
clay biscuits baked
in the moist heat of the sun;

indigestible greens
of okra and kudzu;
the saline sludge
of boiled peanuts;
expanding glut of grits;

their roots work hard
to penetrate your resistant,
cotton-tufted,
tobacco-stained skin;

i bear the indelible
smudge of our every
encounter; i know
the futility of it all:

every seed i ever planted;
every handle from the
shovel head, snapped;

you thwart my northern
expectations; and still,

i love your brash
and fruitful face;
your prophetic battle cry,
"the south will rise again;"

though not as you supposed;
with graceful charm,
and a wealth of opportunity,
the north, you have deposed.

covid

lungs flail,
kick panic
in the deep
bottomless saline
of putrid yellow;

i taste the fabled virus;
swallowing hard a lump
of larynx, bruised
by sharp, angular
obstruction;

my flesh, a holocaust
of burnt offerings, runs
wet with flame; red with chill;

i am consumed, a hollow
shell, in which rattle mere
fractures of lucidity, bare
chunks of insanity;

fever's pitch tightens
the skin of feet
and forehead;

i am become a withered
sack of metallic thirst,
a cracked wineskin of
parched and dry mouth;

in my chest, an ocean
swells to expel the gasps
of drowning shallows;

these ribs constrict
like fists of witless rage,
shattering the oaken thwarts
and collapsing the keel
of my quivering hull;

i go down, seek me no more
among the feckless living;
but, with our final breaths,
exchange with me
forgiveness and forgiving.

Iceland

ice writhes
in agonized veins
of basalt, grinding to dust -
between witless fingers -
the eternal columns of the earth;

rending stone like styrofoam,
glaciers ooze over mountains
in their path, in an ancient
self-possession of turquoise;

while, from below,
the churning sea broods
envy in an unfathomed heart;

where clouds clammer
to ascend slopes of dark
chocolate and pistachio-marbled hills -
higher than the dome of the sky -
weather stalls to drape the coast
in silken green;

still the cotton ball
sheep wander well beyond
the breathless air, waves of wind
tussling their woolen weaves;

what hooves are these
that grip the gravel ground?
what toes might stand

amid such vertical climbs?

movement, joy strewn
lavishly among the pearls
and petals of morning dew,
gallops wild in narrow ellipses –
manes backlit
by the rising sun –
unshod and unfettered
by cares, the purest hearts
speak secrets of an innocent age;

between my toes, sand -
black as ink blots sprung
from a moonless sky -
endures the blows
of an outraged sea;

i whisper alarm to myself,
'i am too much exposed,
this bare and battered earth
is not for me.'

you, and me, and Mia Marie

we returned to the place
where the grass stained our knees,
you, and me, and Mia Marie;

where the bees sipped her drink
and the ants ate our cheese,
you, and me, and Mia Marie;

where questions were asked
and we made her say please,
you, and me, and Mia Marie;

where we talked about Joey
and sweet Meggy Wee,
you, and me, and Mia Marie;

and we laughed to remember
playing games with Andy,
you, and me, and Mia Marie;

when such memories were made
in the soft smiling breeze for
you, and me, and Mia Marie.

Halloween

frost coats the clouds
in powdered sugar,
a dusting of winter
on an autumn day;

glistening in cinnamon crystals
steeped in steaming cider,
my memory stirs
to be teased
by so much fall;

a rain of leaves,
like crayon-colored mittens,
spread wide against the cushioning
breeze, chase endless circles
on the pavement;

i hear their tiny feet -
a million shushing bristles
sweeping clean the dull, grey streets -
mounting up to the sky,
and again, they descend;

the fat pumpkin on my sill is stoic,
as Gracie sits beside its longitudinal
perfection, watching the blue jays
cackle like goblins
in the light of a westering sun;

the gourd is speechless, impassive,

its lines lead from base to stem
in a choreography of silent motion;
its skin pulled taut
over too much flesh;

its seeds, too woody to chew,
fit only for salt and butter
and the once-annual roasting;

i forget, please tell me,
why do we do this each year?

tradition is more sacred
than drops of water
in a baptismal font;

these are rites of initiation,
for the equinox has passed
and the days grow short.

please don't

please don't;
do, be still;
be at peace;
hold your life at bay;
restrain this impulse
to run, to bolt, to dash
yourself to fractured
fragments of a tragedy;
your gentle heart,
no more; your noble frame
crushed by man's
inexorable, blunt force
of careless careening;
i decrease, that you might,
in caution, cross; i slow
the closing of our two
paths; i pause to give you
pause; for your mind
is as unpredictable
as a million variables
of need and want,
skill and desire,
instinct and action,
fear and regret;
oh deer one,
please, don't;
not now, not ever;
but, if it must be,
don't feel in your youth
such final misery.

skin blisters and cracks

skin blisters and cracks,
peeling away from pale flesh still
clinging to ribs of bleached and bruised;

flaking in sinewy strips of wet decay;
the southern sun mars all that is fair;

belly up, it languishes on the sand;
i've half a mind to throw it back,
let the waves have their way;

let salt and surf gnaw
its ragged bones bare;

like dry rot in wormwood,
it yields to the relentless winds;

sifting silt and sawdust
between thumb and forefinger;

slowly surrendering itself beneath the callous
indifference of a sallow-faced sky;

oarless, it founders, with no purpose
but to kindle a fire for roasting clams;

its long memory dashed to pieces on the shore;
abandoned by its owner, evermore, evermore;

and i wonder at its name, *The Weather Eye*;

would it feel its final state fair payment
for a life of labor upon the splintering seas?

for every hook and blade that scarred
its wooden hide? did it sense its doom
approaching on the untimely tide?

or, blindsided by faithless apathy,
did it see, in the end, its noble name belied?

i could speak

i could speak
with you
for hours,
for days
upon weeks
upon years;

even, at times,
employing words,
when lips are not
otherwise engaged;

these hearts have
so much to say;

for, out of a silent
childhood,
across two years
of distant musing,
we then spent
the last year
weaving a heart-song
of unbroken conversation;

and the more i see,
the deeper i long to gaze;

the more i hear,
the greater i yearn to listen;

the closer we touch,
the nearer i wish to draw;

if i could bind myself
to the masthead
of your heart,
i would carve
your image
on the sea;

if i could but
wed your precious heart
then fair and truly
wed would i be.

sometimes, life is a fairy tale

sometimes, life is a fairy tale;
days daydream into drowsy
afternoons; evening paints
an early sunrise;
and all is made new;

tell me, what part
does deserving play,
in all the mysteries
of our lives?

it is a question
without answer;

a circular riddle;

a puzzle not worth puzzling;

i would sooner
dodge such an accounting
than ever be fool enough
to demand my just desserts;

i am too small
for such vast
and weighty things;

i see nothing of the whole;
it is enough to know that
you love me;

for, then are worlds born;
stars collide; all miracles
of ancient renown
hide their eyes
in bashful blushing;

what is it for one man
to walk on water,
when i might
call you my own?

for, if i am young
in your love
then i was destined
to love you
from the day
i was born.

in life's late afternoon, i prayed

in life's late afternoon, i prayed,

'there is still time left in this day;
time to balance the folly of youth;
time to give meaning to pain;
to redeem all that was lost,
and make all things new;
if only,'

i prayed without humility,
without supplication,
i demanded of God,

'if only
You'd send me a heart so formed
in the shape of my unsightly wounds;
if only You'd let me live
what i have learned;
if only You would relent,
it would be an act of wisdom,
to Your credit;
if only You would;
if only.'

but no such love arrived;
none came to answer my prayer;
and the whole economy
of grace, the whole vast, intricate
design of providence seemed
a foolish floundering contraption

careening off the cosmic rails;
swinging freely
in the winds of absurdity;

i could not believe
that life was for
lessons learned;
i do not; i will not;

for what good
is learning
without living?

i am not judged
by what i know,
but by what i do;

' and this doing,
this proving,
You denied me,'
i charged,
taking to task
the One to Whom
i owed my all;

until...

in the cool calm
of surrender,
in the ordered wake
of humility,

i saw Her smile,

and...

our love blossomed to become
the key that unlocked
the storehouse of our hearts;

our minds combined serenely,
like two breezes might
dance to be one;

our souls recognized
their mated purpose,
and knelt before their Maker,
faces to the floor –

two hearts
from one divine flame –

overwhelmed by the hushed
silence of sacred Presence;

and…

in that moment of certainty,

i,
(humbled by all that you are),
whispered my question to you;

and you,
(in sweetness befitting your grace),
whispered your reply,

'yes, yes, yes.'

the trees stagger

the trees stagger,
stepping from their shower,
with long hair
bedraggled and unkempt;
a snarl of snakes matted
to shoulders of timber;
even their trunks
run wet with spring;

under nails, caked brown
and grimy, they squish March
between tuberous toes;
while the frost churns
mudshakes of thick and earthy –
worm sprinkles and butterfly
crunch; winter cravings
are ravenous;

all around them, cattails call;
whistling wanton to the modest
elm, still clinging to her leaves
like a new-fallen Eve;
the wind pranks even the purest;
show me innocence inviolable,
and i will call it a dream;

swollen like a crepe-paper
pom-pom, the soggy hawk
drips haughty in the face
of God; his red tail,

a solitary bruise on a body
of beige, puffed and motionless;

each solitary eye
sweeps the bent
landscape, his brain
making sense of it all;
what prey (tell) would
brave this rain
just to die
at the end of a beak?

swift clouds, like lead balloons
of billowing flab,
entangle themselves
among the branches;
sagging like old age
around the ankles
of alder and ash;
a moment, they glisten
like sugar on the lips,
before the chill,
evening breeze
squanders shapeless
to mist.

i picked a path

i picked a path
through fallen trees;
corpses strewn
across a battlefield
running thick and sloppy
with untyped mud;

i stepped gingerly,
careful to observe
inordinate reverence;
i've always harbored
safe superstitions;
one never knows.

all around: the gore
of a generation
spilt and splattered
in the unkempt grass;

a stern forest's tender youth,
their final springtime
come and gone too soon -
always too soon –

and, powerless to halt
the conquering foe,
decay did win
the sodden field –
triumphant for a time –
to bloat upon fleshless bones;

appalled, the scene affects me
more deeply than the death
of a brother; perhaps
it is the violence of their passing;
or the innocence of their lives;

no matter; impoverished as i am,
i fall to my knees,
among their stripped
and ravaged remains,
to search the ancient senseless
and maybe find a reason why;

there, pinned beneath the stump
of old Alder's skull,
his teeth of jagged
leaves agape,
i found a sapling
crushed and maimed,
its stem hobbled
by the weight of its elders;

and, removing its burden,
i held the broken seedling
in trembling hands,
beneath the wounded sky;

and wept, among
the host of strangers,
to hear its needless
goodbye.

the rusty leaves

the rusty leaves
crumble and flake
into tenuous piles
of shifting dust,
no more than
a powder of pungent
foliage weighed
upon the scale
of springtime;

i, too, was younger
then, but have forgotten
all but summer;

the sky insists upon
wearing nothing
but gaudy blue;

she always did prefer
the cold clarity of autumn,
mourning the long dread
of winter in funeral grey;

why does the sun
not stand his ground?

coward, he is all show
and shine, until he is met
with December;

but see what neglect works
in the frigid folds
of the helpless earth;

come, my love,
let us pack up
our children, our cats,
our poems and sketches,
these rings we so long
to wear;

take one small
leaf for you,
and one broad
leaf for me;

and we'll follow
the warmth
of the unfailing sun
as far as
the southern sea.

from thy birth

when firsts
give way to forevers;

and moments are made
into memories;

in the serenity of tenderness;
in the heart of the home;
in the embrace of love and family;

then do our strivings
bear fruit,
then do our efforts
blossom and bloom;

for, not a drop is wasted,
when we empty ourselves
for those we love;

not a smile or a kind word
falls short of its mark,
when released
from love's bowstring;

in the taut meaning of mindful,
we might weave tapestries -
lives of lights and darks -
all steeped in purpose;
all radiant with worth;

and whisper incessantly
into the hearts and minds
and souls and lives
of our precious children,

"how we have
loved thee
from thy birth."

who am i

who am i
that you
should love me?

who am i
that you
should visit me
from your place
beyond compare?

too real
to wrap myself
around;

too true
to be anything
less than
a dream;

i cannot
behold you,
without seeing
within myself
every shortcoming
sketched in erasable
outlines of smudged
and muddled;

never more than
a study in me;

i have not yet
inked me in;

oh, that i might be
a drawing from
your own hand,
then could i be
what the hidden
in you so
secretly needs;

(and that, before
you yourself knew);

to know and meet
your every need,
would be for me
this dream
come true.

the withered, black pearls

the withered, black pearls
cling to the branch;
dried warts upon
a witch's nose; shriveled
in upon themselves
like the damned,
they have no love left;

even the birds,
in the throes
of winter's want,
pass them by
without a second glance;

they see in them no kindness
to satiate their needs;
they will not break their beaks upon
such useless stones as these;

rank with spite,
they are an obscenity;
a monstrosity
of nature's thwarted purpose;

giving nothing of themselves,
their short lives
dwindle to ruinous
hoarding; all will be
lost by spring;

in the harsh
thirst of desiccation,
i reflect upon my own life,
now nearly spent,
too many fruits of which
hang dead upon the tree;

and i find, in time,
among the fallen leaves,
how stiff and rigid i've become,
a leathered soul beneath
a cruel and thankless sun.

they pass too swiftly

they pass too swiftly,
the minutes to hours,
the sighs from glances,
too brief, and briefer, still,
the closer we draw;

they pass too swiftly,
the smiles between us,
the laughter and tears,
each dawning realization
that we are here at last,
for having come so far;

though time is lost,
consumed by ageless
kisses, wherein we
sip the sweetest
nectar from our souls,
even these will come,
eventually, no more;

they are not long;
they pass
too swiftly
from our hands
then they are gone.

stark realizations

in every assumption,
i have been mistaken;

with every guess,
i have been wrong;

in every assertion,
i approach frail clarity;

with every belief,
i obscure clear sight;

in every doubt,
i bind the hands of action;

with every assurance,
i rediscover faith;

in following reason,
i tangle myself in tangible;

by following my heart,
i free myself for flight.

i would sing to you

i would sing to you
a secret melody, one
of my own devising,
spun like silken threads
through a soft,
falling lace of snow,
and never fear
the ache of endless
winter, ere i go;

i would patch the sky
in tiny, seamless whispers,
hiding cloud behind cloud
behind cloud -
an endless depth
of slate grey
and impartial blue,
until i myself became
the dawn, to break
in rays of selfless
over you;

i would turn my face
skyward, and feel
the wayward rain
trace its wanton fingers
o'er the contours
of my lips, softening
my kiss in the chaste
moonlight; training

my mind in attentive,
my heart in deference,
my soul in reverence
to your sweet,
gentle soul;

i would let these words
dissolve in drops
of meaning, a storm
of striving, a tempest
of yearning, collecting
into puddles
at your feet,
for, even there,
would i love you,
in prostrations,
complete.

let us always be

let us always be
as young as
we are old;

more innocent
than youth;

more liable
to wander off
(hand in hand)
in curiosity
and wonder,
than to sit
in silence,
adrift within
our own thoughts,
just out of reach
of affection;

let us never
lose sight
of sunsets;

grow weary
of miracles;
or forgetful
of you
and me;

let us become

gratitude;

let us bleed
generosity
pale;

let us
love without
boundaries;

and touch
without shame;

let us be
so much one,
that we share
just one name.

let the nighttime enfold us

let the nighttime enfold us
like a quilt, stitched
square by square,
by ancient hands
of knuckles gnarled
and gaunt;

let me pull
the bleak darkness
around our shoulders;

rest your head
upon my chest;
nothing else is
that was;
nothing else was
but this;
nothing speaks nighttime
as softly as these lips
for all you are;

nothing,
no nothing
at all;

beneath the blanket
of this night,
this pinpricked
canvas of timeless
and purple,

of ice pearls
frozen among
flickering fire
in an inky sea,
you breathe;

you breathe,
and the night sky
leans in closer;

for it has never
heard anything
in all its long listening;

never seen anything
in all its eternal perception;

never loved anyone
in all its boundless heartbreak
as delicately beautiful
as you.

i still linger

i still linger
in the wisdom
of unknowing;

i have not yet aged
beyond wonder;
beyond curious;

or waded hip-deep
into the loose-leaf
parchment of belief;

i do not breathe easy
among the dusty shelves
of doctrine, all truth
being black and white -
is not its application
a myriad of grey?

i say it is; and only God
can hope to tease-out
the spaghetti strands
of dense and tangled
hearts; He, and only
He, and that with great effort;

but this, too, is an insensate
fog of unknowing, the drops
of which condense
upon the serrated beak

of a sparrow's final breath;

there is more wisdom there
than in countless wasted
hours; sit awhile, its weightless
head in your hands;

its flightless wings
held cupped against downy
breast; but one in a myriad
hues of truth's grey application;
and i am no wiser for its fall.

we cry more, these days

we cry more, these days;
for, we feel more; see more
clearly, the closer we draw;

de profundis, we move apace;
out of the past, out of ourselves;
we uncover, hidden beneath
the petals of withered
and rootless, wounds
to bind with patient
understanding;

would that i were
a saint, so that i might
be a blessing to you –
as you are, my love, to me;

i have yearned to mingle
my own tears with yours;
to press my cheek against
your sweet face and bathe
my sight in all you see;

my heart in saline seas
of you; i do not fear
these depths,
for their peaks and valleys
correspond to the subtle
fall of my canyons;

open to receive the heights
of my assertions;

and always your currents
shape the shifting sands
of my soul's stony bed;

whence these healing
springs arise?
their waters burst forth
from cracks made
by every embrace;

chest pressed to chest,
our hearts long to pass
their days together,
but cannot endure the steady
beating of the jealous moon;

nighttime begs for more;
morning clings to nighttime;
and each caress becomes
cause for cathartic cleansing;

tears of our hearts' espousal;
soft rains for wildflower meadows;
and wine for our wedding day
when, with trembling hands
and grateful joy,
every tear will be
wiped away.

do you remember

do you remember
the first time
i held your hand
in mine?

i thought it best
to ask forgiveness
than permission,
life being short and
love being
an uncertain thing;

and how each
sweep and swirl
of your fingerprints fit
like interlocking
puzzle pieces
with my own,
as if you'd
always been mine;

one singular creation,
forged from the same mold;
and, if twin flames,
then there never was
a time when you
were not mine
(or i yours, forever,
and from before the first
movement of time);

feel again how i pressed
each finger to my lips;
one hand on the wheel,
the other sat softly
on your heart;
steering us
toward paths unknown;

i fell in love with you,
smile by soul by fingertips
by mind by kiss by heart
by leaps and bounds, unbridled;

by every touch between;
by every moment spent;
by every word revealing
the unexpected interwoven
twists of yearning for what
we could not even imagine;

life being long
and love being
an unfathomable thing;

but is this
not your hand
still here
in mine?

the cardinal puffs

the cardinal puffs
his plumage like a pout;
it's been a long winter
among the muddy meadows;

since spring has just arrived,
the southern sun now sucks
the puddles dry;

but he's just in time;
the sluggish rainwater runs
brown from his breast;

i half expect his scruffy feathers
to bleed red;
the white, winter sky
has bleached him so;

the earthworms emerge
braver than i recall;
or is it that the rain has floated
all their fears away,
their cautious concerns,
their homes and all
their worm-worn trinkets?

with nothing left to lose,
they risk it all,
and count it very little,
beneath a perilous sky;

i've known such disregard before;

who will clean up
all this stale and useless?
last year's clothing
cast down and tossed aside;
is it not wasteful
to wear only once?

there's barely room allowed
for the newborn leaves,
who arrange,
with helpless hands,
the dry bones of the old;
their bodies not yet cold;
nor this my languid soul;
nor this my languid soul.

angel on a tombstone

how many sunsets
your eyes have seen;
how many nightfalls;
how many mourners
clapped in grief
like prisoners of woe;

how many passings
hence, you've known;
is this why
your eyes are closed?
it's all too much and,
now, no more;

the flowers you strew
are all but gone;
your gaze
averts sorrow;
your gaze
sweeps the ground
where countless souls
have gone before;
and, doubtless, more
await their sowing;

in this field of remembrance;
this meadow of hope;
with hand outstretched,
you crown the slope
where sunrise treads with awe.

spring's first butterfly

with what words
might i speak
your beauty?

with what wonder
might i comprehend?
how deftly you wear
strength's splendor,
beneath a veil
of subtle innocence;
too delicate
for these hands to hold;

but, how i long to possess you;
to give you wings;
to see you soar;
that, free to choose,
you might choose me;

for, is this not the paradox of love?
that grasping loses all we seek,
while giving gains the world;
if only i had something to give you
for you lack nothing i possess;

these eyes could caress
your form for a lifetime;

an infinite inexhaustible
of excruciating grace;

each curve of your feminine;
each shape and shade
of your chaste;
the every contour
of life's consequence,
drawn in
and spoken again
from a heart
made more
perfectly you;

but, hush...
i will calm my restless
wandering of words
upon the breeze;

for your soul is more beautiful
than spring's first butterfly
at play among the trees.

the old guard sleeps

the old guard sleeps
at the gates
of our hearts;

worn weapons scattered
just out of reach
of former defenses;

together, we are
on our own;
vulnerable
to the dangers
of love and wild discovery;

without walls to enclose
or pits to ensnare
the wolves who once wore
innocence like primeval
leaves of fig
and ancient deception;

barely were their sins
concealed; we have felt
their ragged teeth
in our tender flesh, of old;

but never again,
for we are
and that is more
than enough to sate

these sacred sighs;

i am but a fringe,
a thin outline,
a scant borderland
at whose core yawns
profound vacancy
in the shape
of your abundant
all and every aspect;
only you
could fit the naught
at the heart of me;

only you could
so exceed my every need,
before ever i know them,
you are;

before ever i look,
you see;

before ever you were,
you were you
for me;

who could hope to heal,
but by the Hand of God?

who could unstack stone
from heavy stone,
except by Strength Divine?

who could move
from caution

through trust,
and well beyond?

casting aside
such contractual
terms in lieu
of covenant truths;
you for me,
and i for(ever) you;

farewell to arms,
we bid thee adieu;
the old perilous world
is withered
and swept away,
in the golden light
of love's first day.

step not

step not
where shadows darken
the fallen snow;

where memory moans
beneath the weight
of too much winter;

where what was
once innocence,
pure and untrodden,
now browns
amid the muddy mire;

is it not ironic?
is it not a shame?
that some things
lose themselves
completely
in shadows cast
by falling rain;

i am one;
i, too, am one;

for, if the chaste
and virtuous snow
cannot bear
such sullen scrutiny,
what hope have we?

we are undone; 'tis true,
we are undone; beneath
the full, fair face
of the midday sun;

we are,
all and every
one, undone;

and, curling, the sun
corrupts this outer shell,
until, all that is left,
that, too, is gone;

and sagging,
dripping,
rivulets run
above our heads,
and, thence, below,
from where
the shadows darken
the fallen snow.

finding truth in suffering

we can not
hold onto passing things
with fleeting, ephemeral fingers;
these hands of mine
are (even now)
passing away;

for, all is ash;
all is dust;
and all that lives
must die;

these breaths
we breathe,
these sighs
and whispers,
these un-ghostly
vapors haunting
the halls
of our souls
are precious,
essential things;

shared and rationed;
portioned-out;
used and reused;
at first
by me,
and then
by you,

and then
by someone
new;

in just such a way
as this, does death
set the stage for life;
in just such a way,
is life indebted
to its own demise;

and yet,
this closed system;
this efficient, excruciating
economy of existence
is fraught
with meaning,
and labors in love
to give birth
to beauty;

it seems
that irony
is life's
literary device;

it gives me pause...

for, if this is true,
then i disdain
fair death
without
just cause.

they are strangers

they are strangers,
these names and titles;
these public figures;
these celebrities, obscure;
they are but flesh and bone,
beneath the facade
of famous, the lies of renown;
and i do not know them;

so why would i prefer them
over you? my brother, my sister,
my could-be-friend?

do i, rather, trust myself
to politics, to persona,
to the cult of personality?

can i look them in the eye;
hold them to their word;
or size-up their sincerity?

how could a stranger
be more real to me
than the neighbor
i, everywhere, see?

change of plan

i do not fear
a change of plan;

all is
as it should be;

all is
as it was
ever meant to be;

all is
in the Maker's hands;

i fear only
the false sense
of security,
of being
in command
of my destiny,
or yours,
or any living being's;

falls from such heights
only ever end
in disillusionment;

but if we can dilate
our hearts well beyond
their widest smile;

if we can pause,
to let joy catch up,
for a while;

then might we laugh,
in spite of all fear,
for the change of plan
that brought
two hearts
ever near.

winter breathes morning

winter breathes morning
upon a pane of dank
and drowsy;

i yearn
only to lay abed,
pulling the warm
air over my head
like a Saturday
in springtime;

mother calls to me,
her voice drips
understanding;

her words, shaped
by lips that love me
more than morning
loves the dawn;

and, too soon,
we are gone;

off to greet the day;

off, exchanging waves
with those who wait
to whisper,
'you are loved;'

and so we are;

and, somehow,
i can see beyond
this morning veil
of one day more
before the longed for lull;

as sunrise paints
itself across
the sky so pale.

On a stranger's sadness

once, i walked
the narrow darkness;
alone, i felt
the curved
and crushing
fist of fingerless
despair;

all had fallen
to ruinous ash,
lifted high
upon the thieving winds
billowing like raw
hurricanes of ignorance
from heedless tongues,
and scattered
to the unfathomed sea;

once, i was
as you are now;
once, you might say,
you were me;

and yet, we can no more
compare two sufferings
than we could one soul
to another, each being
a species unto itself;
each being a blade
of jagged me, tailored

to the tender textures
of the heart;

there are no words
of consolation;
no helpful adage;
no encouraging hope
to lay claim to in the night;

only this, and this is all:
that you are not alone;

though trussed
and tangled-up
in threads
of fate's own weaving,
you need not tease
apart the unyielding
strings with solitary
strivings;
you are not alone;

though grown accustomed
more to brokenness
than you ever
once felt whole;
you are not alone;
you are not alone;

no, i will not encumber you
by waiting on a word
that might never come;

with placing frail hopes
in trembling hands;

by asking greater strength
of one so weary;

let me only sit awhile
in your sorrow,

as the night grows warm
with the faint hope of tomorrow.

the meadow wears wet

the meadow wears wet
and matted lion's mane,
coarse as harsh December;
tumbling down a patchwork sky
of quilted and smooth,
the rain tussles ruinous;
even spring might
never be the same;

i trace the paths of the rain;
countless rivulets wandering
among the sodden feet
of stalks and sumac;
what is it that they seek,
beyond a frenzied
path to the sea?
where awaits
freedom and the quiet
of sheer oblivion;

the earth yields its treasures,
dissolved in a slurry
of slow decay;
hidden in plain view
beneath a blanket of loam;
i think, only the rain
could gnaw iron
or drink sulfurous;
only water could subdue
the fruitful earth;

the tall grass sweats
chaos in the steam of sunrise;
each droplet, an uncut gem
encrusting ragged,
auburn breeches;
elongated forms,
drawn grotesque
by the sinuous hands
of the morning,
stilt and falter
through the swampy slog;

i brush the earth's white
hair aside, feel the chill
of thick dew on my fingernails –
made thin as tissue by the mist;

inhaling the scent
of belonging,
i hear my heartbeat
in the patter
of the falling rain;

for neither spring
nor i
will ever be
the same.

feel the brevity of life

feel the brevity of life,
as i have from my youth;
the tight grip of urgent;
the shallow gasp of fleeting;

are we not in haste?
do we not fail
to outpace the inevitable?
are we not dogged by death?

at the bottom of this hill
of brakeless unstoppable,
a brick wall looms
against frail
mortality;
a hard stop
against hope;
there is no padding,
no safe conduct,
no avoiding
the soul's release;

my hands are too slick
with effluent dismay
to grasp this final doom;

but it is there,
always there;
i fear it not,
damned bully;

oh where is thy victory?
oh where is thy sting?

this is not the end
of all things, only all
that i have known;
and this i whom
i have known;
this me who was mine,
though given,
as i was to you;
i do so regret
your loss of me;

this is not morbid dread;
i do not pity my lot; no,
this is a clarion call;
a warning reminder
that time does not age,
but dies more readily
than it was born;

therefore, make no plans,
for there is no tomorrow,
only today in which to live
all love, all joy, all sorrow.

i have written

i have written
tens of thousands
of words for you,
but have yet
to pen your heart;

i have woven
melodies
from the fibers
of purest desire,
but have yet
to sing your smile;

i have sought beauty
in the face of the sky,
but have yet
to find beauty
greater than thine.

a scribble of orange crayon

a scribble of orange crayon
across a sky of textured
and drawn; curving inward
upon itself, embracing
its own lonely;
it's own every;
its own peculiar identity;
for who is like the sky?

i watch the dizzying-slow
spectacle unravel another day;
a ball of yarn batted about
by the soft paws of evening;
spaghetti strings unwound,
let's gather them up for remembrance;

if i could lick the sky, SweeTart tang
of faded citrus; tastebuds burst
across horizons of sudden savoring;
i'd break off a thin piece for you;
legs tangled in the cool grass,
your hand against my lips;
a sweet remedy for sour sunsets;

reaching heavenward, i scratch
with the nail of forefinger and fancy,
loosening a fleck of orange from above;
and i wonder, were you and i made
for sunsets? or were sunsets made
for our love?

About the Poet

Matt Pelicano was born near Syracuse, New York and by age 10 was already writing poems, songs, and stories.

At the age of 17, Matt published his first compilation of poetry, followed by a second a year later. At age 18, Matt's poetry was featured with a centerfold spread in the *New York Span* and numerous inclusions in the monthly poetry journal, *Omnific*.

One of Matt's children's books, *Philbert LaRue had a Hole in his Shoe*, has been compared with the works of Dr. Seuss and Shel Silverstein. The second of Matt's novels, the result of almost two years-worth of onsite research in France, *A Butterfly in Paris,* is an adventure story, a travel guide, and a French language primer all rolled into one.

Matt's first novel, *Tabouli: The Story of a Heart-Driven Diabetes Alert Dog,* seeks to raise awareness of diabetes alert dogs and the vital work they perform, while encouraging those suffering with juvenile diabetes to always *"follow the adventure"* and live life to the fullest.

Recommended by world-renown dog trainer, Debby Kay, "*Tabouli* perfectly captures the spirit and journey of a remarkable service dog." *Tabouli* has been nominated for three awards by the Dog Writer's Association of America and was optioned by a major television network for adaptation into a made-for-tv movie.

Matt's third novel, written for a more mature readership, is an extended allegorical journey through the various stages of grief. Drawing upon his own experience, *The Woolems of Averlune,* addresses suffering and hopelessness with an eye toward healing and regaining a sense of joy.

Matt has received nationwide media attention for his writing. Some of this press coverage can be seen on his website: www.MattPelicano.com.

From his youth, Matt has always loved the poetry of E.E. Cummings, Shel Silverstein, TS Eliot, Walt Whitman, Robert Frost, and William Shakespeare. His literary heroes include JRR Tolkien, CS Lewis, Oscar Wilde, Agatha Christie and David McCullough.

Matt has three grown children — Andy, Joey and Megan - and lives in New York and South Carolina.

www.ingramcontent.com/pod-product-compliance
Lightning Source LLC
Chambersburg PA
CBHW031451160726
47994CB00005B/1973